ORIENTAL RUGS

ORIENTAL RUGS

The Illustrated Guide

BY

JANICE SUMMERS HERBERT

with Photographs by Richard M. LeNoir

MACMILLAN PUBLISHING CO., INC.

NEW YORK

COLLIER MACMILLAN PUBLISHERS

LONDON

Macmillan Publishing Co., Inc.
866 Third Avenue, New York, N.Y. 10022
Collier Macmillan Canada, Ltd.

Library of Congress Cataloging in Publication Data
Herbert, Janice Summers.
 Oriental rugs.
 1. Rugs, Oriental. I. Title.
NK2808.H52   746.7'5   77-19201
ISBN 0-02-551120-3

Designed by Philip Grushkin

Second Printing 1978
Printed in the United States of America

CONTENTS

To my mother
Katherine Case Summers
with Love

ACKNOWLEDGMENTS

I am grateful for my friends who have given their encouragement while I worked on this book. A special thank you is extended to those who graciously offered their rugs for the illustrations.

My deep appreciation goes to Mr. Abdolrahim Etessami of Tehran, Iran, for all of his advice and assistance. My gratitude goes to Forshad and Farzan Etessami of Alfandari and Etessami Company, Inc., and especially to Kamran Etessami for all his cooperation and kindness shown me.

I am forever indebted to Richard LeNoir for the long hours and hard work he devoted, without which the superb rug photographs would not have been possible. The value of his contributions and friendship are inestimable. And to his wife Carolyn go my thanks for all of her support.

My husband has shared with me the tears and joys, and without his understanding and encouragement this manuscript could not have been written. To him go my deep love and appreciation.

Jeanne Fredericks, my editor at Macmillan, has been a wonderful person with whom to work; for her advice and help I thank her.

A. & J. ETESSAMI

(ALIZADEH)

Export & Commission Agents

ORIENTAL CARPETS & RUGS

Partners :

Abdolrahim Etessami

Jahangir Etessami

Cable : ALLIOFF

Phone { Office 20911 / Home 42740

TEHERAN, Iran

Saray Bouali

At long last a book is available which shows today's
Oriental rugs rather than priceless museum pieces. Mrs.Herbert
has made a substantial contribution to those who wish to have
expert advice on what they can reasonably expect to see and
obtain in an Oriental rug.

As one of the most knowledgeable people in the field,
she is eminently qualified to do so. Her experience and
integrity as a lecturer, dealer, and collector show quite
clearly in the thoroughness with which she has organized what
is the only book of its kind. Her research and extensive
travels to the major rug-weaving centers of the world give
her book an authoritativeness and perspective unique in its
field.

Readers will find this book an indispensable aid. It
is especially valuable for those who wish to know what choices
they really have in Oriental rugs, identify and evaluate those
rugs that have puzzled them for years, learn about rugs as
an historic art form, and find out practical tips on buying
and caring for their rugs.

Her book is a valuable reference for beginner and dealer
alike. Readers could do no better than to have Mrs. Herbert
as a concerned and expert guide through this complex subject.

A. Etessami
Tehran

A. Etessami

1

Introduction to Oriental Rugs

FEW ART FORMS are surrounded with the aura of mystique that is associated with Oriental rugs. The entire subject has become romanticized to the extent that those interested in Oriental rugs have a great deal of difficulty separating fact from fancy. Those who undertake the study of Oriental rugs can quickly fall prey to an overwhelming and bewildering amount of highly technical information. My aim is to provide a comprehensible review of the rugs most likely to be found, and sound advice on their purchase and care.

The term "Oriental rug" refers specifically to handmade (both knotted and woven) rugs from Iran, Turkey, the Caucasus regions of Russia, China, Turkestan (both east and west), India, and Pakistan. A relatively small number of Oriental rugs are also made in Rumania and Japan. Machine-made rugs of an "Oriental" design are *not* Oriental rugs.

An Oriental rug is an art form, but one need not be an expert or connoisseur to appreciate and admire its beauty. As with any other art form, taste and preference are important; each rug is a uniquely individual expression of creativity—in a utilitarian form—and must be evaluated on its own merits. There are some general guides and procedures that one can follow in developing an informed evaluation and appreciation of Oriental rugs. We can group these as considerations of rug construction, design, origin, and evaluation; each of these is covered in a major section of this book.

An Historical Overview

No one knows exactly when or where the first hand-knotted carpets were made. The oldest example, known as the Pazyryk carpet, was found in southern Siberia in the Altai Mountain valley of Pazyryk. This carpet is approximately 2,500 years old. It has a panel-type design and five separate borders; one border consists of reindeer figures and another has men on horseback. Its pile was knotted with the Turkish knot.

Carved on a relief at Persepolis, dating back 2,500 years, is an ambassador presenting rugs as a gift to the Persian king. Fifth and sixth century A.D. carpet fragments have been found along the old caravan routes in the eastern Turkestan region.

In many fourteenth- and fifteenth-century European paintings, by Martini, Carpaccio, and Lorenzo de Credi, Oriental rugs are depicted. Hans

PLATE 1: *Stone relief at Persepolis, showing the presentation of Oriental rugs to the Persian king.*

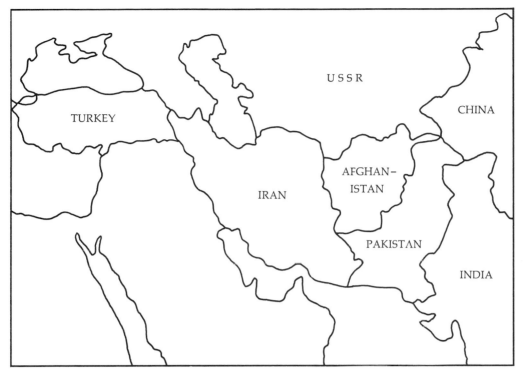

FIGURE 1: *RUG-WEAVING COUNTRIES OF THE WORLD*

Holbein the Younger, in the sixteenth century, painted masterpieces with Oriental rugs detailed in their backgrounds; these rugs have come to be known as the Holbein carpets. Since no part of these carpets remain today, pictorial evidence has proven extremely important in gathering information on rug-making history.

The oldest Persian carpet fragment dates to the sixteenth century. However, there are Arab references to carpets of the Fars region of Persia in the ninth century. Persian carpets are pictured in miniatures of the fourteenth century from both Shiraz and northeastern Persia. The floors in the palace of Ghazan Khan were said to have been covered with carpets from Fars.

Under the Safavid rulers (1499–1722) the Persian arts as a whole had a renaissance. Of these rulers, Shah Abbas the Great (1587–1629) was the patron of the carpet industry. In 1590, Shah Abbas moved his capital to Isfahan, where he established workshops for the designers and weavers to create carpet masterpieces. After his death, the art of carpet-making declined steadily until the Afghan invasion in 1722, when the last remnants of the art were virtually destroyed. Very little carpet-making was done for the next 150 years.

During the last quarter of the nineteenth century, carpet-making was again reborn. Merchants from Tabriz set up looms for the making of carpets to meet the increasing interest and demand in Europe. Since that time, with only a few minor setbacks, carpet-making has had a steady increase in popularity and demand.

Rug-Weaving Today

Recent changes in laws and industrial development have profoundly changed the nature of the Iranian carpet-weaving industry. Compulsory education has been instituted for all children, who were once relied upon for a portion of the weaving process. Shah Mohammed Reza Pahlavi has reinvested billions of oil revenue dollars into crash programs to industrialize and diversify Iran's economy. As a result, industrial competition from alternative employment sources has driven up wage rates, and has siphoned off the pool of weaving labor into other industries. Wage rates have also risen because weaving is a labor-intensive process—an average 4-by-6-foot rug will take one skilled weaver a year or more to complete.

The cost of raw materials used in the weaving of rugs has also soared. The decreasing weaving labor supply, rising wage rates, and increasing prices for raw material have combined to make Oriental rugs one of today's best investments.

Construction

ALL ORIENTAL RUGS are hand-knotted on a webbing formed by the warp and weft threads. Attached to the top and bottom of the loom, *warp* threads run vertically through the carpet. A strand of wool is tied to a pair of warp threads, forming a knot. The loose ends of the knots, which make up the body of the rug, are called *pile. Weft* threads run horizontally through the carpet and are used to secure the knots; one way to remember the difference between warp and weft threads is that wefts go from "weft" to right, not up and down.

Weaving Process

The weaver sits facing a loom upon which the warp threads are strung, while overhead are balls of colored yarn to be used in the rug. Reaching up, the weaver takes the end of a strand of spun wool, ties it across a pair of warp threads, and cuts free the end of the strand that is still attached to the ball of yarn. Tying and cutting the wool is done in one swift motion. So skilled are the weavers that, like the hands of a magician, their fingers move so deftly that the eye cannot follow them.

After each row of knots has been completed, one or more weft threads are woven in and out of each warp thread. To secure them firmly in place, the weft threads and knots are beaten down with a "comb." Any excess knotted yarn is trimmed with a large pair of scissors after each row of knots. (In some areas, this may be done after the carpet has been completed.) The weaver repeats this operation hundreds of times until the carpet has been completed.

Designs are formed by the arrangement of different-colored knotted yarns. The placement of each knot may be directed or specified in several different ways. The nomadic weaver, for example, is usually a woman,

PLATE 2: *Cartoon*

who weaves a carpet from patterns learned from her mother or from forms unique to her own tribe. The urban or semi-urban weaver may be a woman, a man, or even a child; this weaver has a section of a drawing (called a *cartoon* or *talim*) from which to work. These cartoons are usually drawn to scale with a single square on the piece of paper indicating each knot. The design is colored and cut in horizontal strips, then either placed in a plastic casing for protection or mounted on a board and varnished.

Carpets are finished in one of several different ways; the warp threads may be knotted and cut to form a fringe, a *kelim*, or a combination of the two. A *kelim* is a strip of cloth formed by weaving the weft threads back and forth through the warp threads. The selvedges, or the sides, of the carpet are secured and reinforced, generally by taking the last few warp threads and wrapping them tightly with an extra weft thread. Each weaving center has its own unique manner of securing the selvedge; these various processes will be discussed when the individual rugs are described.

Looms

There are two classifications of looms: the ground or horizontal loom and the upright or vertical loom. There are three types of vertical looms: the

PLATE 3: *Tabriz weavers at loom*

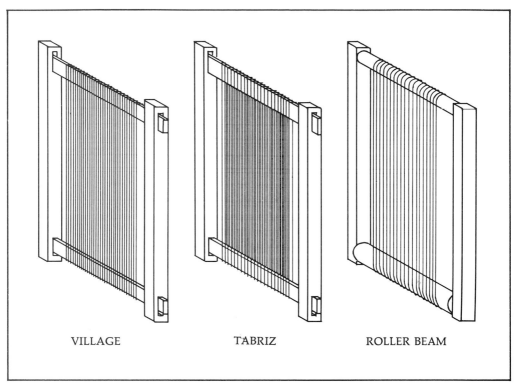

FIGURE 2. *LOOMS*

village type, the Tabriz type, and the roller beam type, all shown in Figure 2.

The *ground* or *horizontal loom* is the simplest of the looms. Because it is easily collapsed and moved from place to place, it is used by nomadic tribes, some seminomadic tribes, and villagers. The warp threads are fastened to upper and lower beams, which are held in place by stakes driven into the ground. When the nomads are ready to move, the stakes are removed, and the unfinished carpet is rolled around one of the beams. Once resettled, the carpet is unrolled, the stakes reset, and the weaving process begun again.

The simplest of the *vertical* looms is the *village type*. The weaver sits on a plank which is raised or lowered, always enabling the weaver to sit directly in front of the area of the carpet on which she is working. The warp threads are attached to the upper and lower beams of a simple frame. Although the length of the carpet is usually only as long as the distance between the upper and lower beams, it is possible to make the carpet longer by a complicated process. In this procedure, the warp threads are loosened and the completed part of the rug is reattached to the lower beam. The warp threads are then retightened on the upper beam, and the weaving process is continued.

The *Tabriz type* of loom, so named because it originated in Tabriz, is a little more complicated than the village type. The warp threads pass in a continuous loop around the upper and lower beams. Slack in the warp threads is taken up by driving wedges in the space where the side supports meet the lower beam. The weavers do not have to be raised with this type of loom because, as the weaving process progresses, the rug is lowered down around the lower beam and up the back of the loom. The completed part of the carpet then can be easily inspected. With this type of loom, the carpet can be as long as twice the distance between the upper and lower beams (see Plate 3.)

The *roller beam type* is the most advanced of the looms. The warp threads are wound around the upper beam, leaving the ends attached to the lower beam. As the weaving progresses, the warp threads are unwound from the upper beam and the finished part of the carpet is rolled around the lower beam. It is easy to weave carpets of any length on this loom. In addition, the tension of the warps is adjusted by rotating the beams, producing a straighter carpet. Looms of this type are used in Kerman.

Materials

Cotton and wool are the most important materials used in the creation of Oriental rugs. Silk is also used, though its expense limits its use. The use of cotton and wool depends largely on their availability. The warp and weft threads of most Persian and Chinese rugs are cotton, whereas those of most Caucasian and Turkoman rugs are wool. The pile of Oriental rugs is generally wool. The exception to the rule is the silk rug; warp, weft, and pile are all made of silk.

Cotton is a better fiber for the warp and weft threads than wool. It does not possess the elastic tendencies of wool and knots can be tied tighter to a cotton warp, yielding a more closely woven carpet. Rugs made with a cotton warp and weft are also heavier than those made of wool; as a result they lie flatter on the floor and will not "walk" or "creep." Silk is the strongest fiber used for warp threads because of its tensile strength. The most finely knotted rugs are woven with silk warp threads.

Wools vary greatly from region to region. Many different factors affect texture, color, quality, and durability, including breed of sheep, climate, and time of year in which the wool is shorn (either fall or spring). For example, sheep raised in the mountain areas have heavier and thicker wool than sheep raised in the desert. Because wools vary so greatly, the characteristics will be discussed with each type of rug.

Silk has been used in the making of carpets since the earliest of times. Very few silk rugs are woven today for several reasons. First, the silk itself is very expensive; and second, because silk pile does not wear particularly

PLATE 4: *Tying knot with Tabriz hook*

well, its use has been restricted largely to rugs for decorative purposes, such as wall hangings.

In recent years, mercerized cotton has been developed which, when woven in a rug, resembles silk so closely that it is hard to tell the difference. The use of mercerized cotton is common in Turkish and some Turkoman rugs, and these rugs have often been represented to unsuspecting buyers as silk. Murray Eiland* suggests the best way to tell the difference is to wet a small portion of the rug; the wet mercerized cotton will feel more like ordinary cotton, and the silk rug will retain its silky feel.

Goat's hair and camel's hair are occasionally encountered in Oriental rugs. The Qashqai, Balouchi, and Afghans use goat's hair for selvedges and, on occasion, for warp and weft threads. Many people believe that the caramel-colored wool found in Hamadan and Kurd rugs is camel's hair. Because of its expense, camel's hair was rarely used in the past and is now almost never employed. The camel color found in most rugs is from sheep's wool that has been dyed with walnut husks. Camel's hair possesses a definite odor when wet.

There is a practice in which the wool of butchered sheep ("skin" or "dead" wool) is used. The animal skin is submerged in a caustic solution

---

* Murray Eiland, *Oriental Rugs: A Comprehensive Guide* (Greenwich, Conn.: New York Graphic Society, Ltd., 1973), p. 25.

which allows the wool to be easily scraped from the skin. This process, however, weakens the woolen fibers, and rugs made with this wool will wear much faster than those made with wool shorn from living sheep. Also, skin wool takes dyes poorly and gives a carpet a dull and lusterless appearance. With experience, skin wool can be readily detected; skin wool feels comparatively coarse and bristly to the touch.

Knots

The spun wool may be tied to the warp threads in two different ways, either by a Turkish (Ghiordes) or a Persian (Senna) knot (see Figure 3). Though the tying technique of these types of knots may vary slightly from region to region, the end result is the same.

The nomenclature is somewhat confusing and can be misleading. For example, some authors refer to the Persian knot as the Senna knot (named after the ancient town of Senna). However, the rugs made in Senna are woven with the Turkish knot and never with the Senna knot. The Turkish knot is sometimes called the Ghiordes knot, named for the small town of Ghiordes in the western Anatolian plateau of Turkey. Yet this knot is used not only in Ghiordes, but in almost all of Turkey, in all of Caucasia, and in many tribal and village areas of Iran. Turks and Turki-speaking

PLATE 5: *Securing weft thread with comb*

peoples usually employ the Turkish knot, regardless of the tribe's location. Persian and Farsi-speaking peoples weave with the Persian knot.

The *Turkish knot* is a strand of wool that encircles two warp threads, with the loose ends drawn tightly between the two warps. This is the easiest knot to tie, but also the coarsest.

The *Persian knot* is a strand of wool that encircles one warp thread and winds loosely around the other. One loose end is pulled through the two warp threads, while the other emerges outside of the paired warps. Although the more difficult of the two types to tie, the Persian knot gives a more clearly defined pattern and a more tightly woven rug.

The *jufti*, or *"false,"* *knot* is simply a Turkish or Persian knot tied to four warp threads instead of two. The use of the *jufti* knot has spread through the carpet industry in epidemic proportions. Using this knot enables the weavers to tie only half as many knots as would be normally required if using the Turkish or Persian knot. Since four warp threads are

PLATE 6: *Tools used in rugmaking*

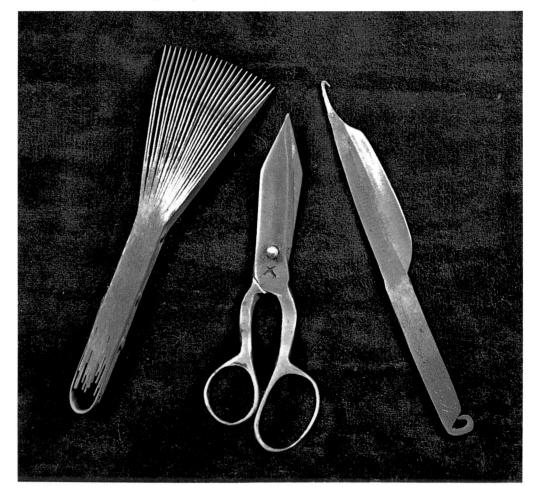

Cross section

Warps on same level

TURKISH
KNOT

Depressed warp

Cross section

PERSIAN KNOT

Cross section

TURKISH JUFTI KNOT

Cross section

PERSIAN JUFTI KNOT

FIGURE 3: *KNOTS*

used instead of two, a carpet may be woven with half the number of knots in half the time. Pile density is halved, however, which weakens the carpet and causes it to wear faster.

Dyes

The dyeing process is a delicate and complicated one. The procedure may vary slightly, depending on the substance used in making the dye. Basically, the wool is chemically treated to make it more receptive to the dye and then submerged in a vat full of dye. The length of time the wool stays in the vat depends upon the type of dye and the hue desired, and may last as long as a few hours to a few days. When the desired color has been attained, the wool is removed and spread in the sun to dry.

There are three types of dyes that have been used in the dyeing of Oriental rugs: natural vegetable and animal, aniline, and chrome. Aniline and chrome are synthetic dyes.

NATURAL VEGETABLE AND ANIMAL DYES

Making and using the natural vegetable dyes is time-consuming and can be quite expensive. The colors are derived from a number of different sources:

madder red—root of the madder plant
cochineal red—cochineal insect
yellow—weld, vine leaves, or pomegranate peel
brown—walnut shells or oak bark
orange—henna leaves
blue—indigo plant
green—combination of weld and indigo

In older rugs there is often a slight change of color which will run horizontally through the field of the carpet. This is called an *abrash*. It occurs because the yarn is sometimes dyed in small batches, and because, especially with vegetable dyes, it is hard to obtain an exact match in color between different dye lots. The *abrash* is created when the weaver begins using yarn from a dye lot that does not exactly match the dye lot previously employed. This is not objectionable in itself and does not affect the quality of the rug.

ANILINE DYES

The use of aniline dyes was introduced to the carpet industry in the latter half of the nineteenth century. Being easier and cheaper to use, these dyes were adopted all too readily. They were usually strongly acidic, which destroyed the natural oil in the wool, thus weakening the pile and causing it to wear rapidly. The colors not only faded when exposed to sunlight, but ran when washed. These dyes damaged the rug industry so severely that the Persian government passed laws in the 1890s prohibiting their importation and use. Inferior chemical dyes are still used in some bazaar-quality Turkish rugs. Aniline-dyed rugs are easily recognized by their faded colors; the back is much brighter than the sunlight-faded front.

CHROME DYES

Most rugs are now dyed with what are commonly referred to as "chrome dyes," synthetic dyes treated with potassium bichromate. In contrast to the natural dyes, chrome dyes are much simpler to prepare and their dye lots easier to match. These dyes provide a wider variety of shades, are colorfast, and will not fade when exposed to sunlight or washed with water or an alkaline solution. The natural oils of the wool are not removed by the dyes, so the wearing qualities of the rug are not impaired.

The major complaint about chrome dyes has been that their colors are harsher than the mellow hues of natural dyes, a problem which has been corrected by the use of a light chemical wash. Too often the imperfections of natural dyes are forgotten. For example, oak bark, which was used to make black and brown dyes, contained iron salts which weakened woolen fibers and caused them to wear rapidly.

Washing and Painting

For several decades (1920 to 1940), the colors of new Persian rugs were too bright for the expanding U.S. market. Rugs were given a rather heavy chemical wash to tone down what Americans thought were harsh colors, such as bright red. While the heavy wash did subdue the colors, it also removed the natural oils from the woolen pile fibers, greatly reducing the rug's life-span. Over a period of time, the heavy wash also destroyed the warp and weft threads. When the rug was folded, its foundation actually cracked or broke.

Washing reduced the brilliant color contrasts within a rug, turning the red ground into a rather drab muted pinkish rose. Since the darker reds, especially maroon, were particularly appealing to American tastes, a painting process was initiated. The washed ground color was colored or "painted" by a hand-applied dye. Another process was then necessary to add the desired luster or sheen to the rug. Almost all Sarouks imported during this period were both washed and painted, as were some Dergazines and Lillihans.

3

Design

THE DESIGNS AND VARIATIONS in Oriental rugs are so numerous that it would be impossible to describe them all. These variations in design occur in the two main parts of the rug: the *field* (or *ground*) and the *borders*, which frame the interior (the field of the carpet). Designs fall into two different categories: curvilinear and rectilinear (see Plates 7 and 8). *Curvilinear* designs have floral motifs and patterns, with curved outlines and tendrils; *rectilinear* designs have geometric or angular motifs and patterns. Both of these categories are classified by the type of design or pattern which occupies the field: medallion, repeated motif, all-over, and prayer.

Medallion

The medallion rug will have a field which is dominated by a central medallion or by several medallions. The field surrounding the medallion may be "open" (empty) or semi-open (filled with detached floral sprays or other small motifs).

Repeated Motif

In a repeated design, the central field is filled with multiple rows of the same motif. Among the repeated designs are the Mina Khani, Guli Henna, Herati, Zil-i-soltan, Boteh, and Gul patterns.

MINA KHANI

The Mina Khani design is comprised of repeated floral motifs, each of which is surrounded by four similar smaller flowers, joined in turn by

PLATE 7: *RECTILINEAR (Tabriz)*   PLATE 8: *CURVILINEAR (Tabriz)*

vines to form a diamond arrangement. The design is found in older Bijars, occasionally in Hamadans and Kurds, and quite often in the Veramin (see Figure 4).

GULI HENNA

Guli Henna (henna flower) has small yellow plantlike motifs which resemble stalks with many flowers and leaves, and are set in rows; each motif is contained within a diamond-shaped bouquet. This pattern is most often used in older rugs from the Hamadan and the Sultanabad areas (see Figure 4).

HERATI

The Herati pattern is the design used most often in the Persian rugs. It consists of a rosette surrounded by four leaves or "fish" and generally, though not necessarily, found inside a diamond shape ("lozenge"). Bijar, Ferahan, and Hamadan weave the Herati design with the diamond; Khurasan weaves it without the diamond (see Figure 4).

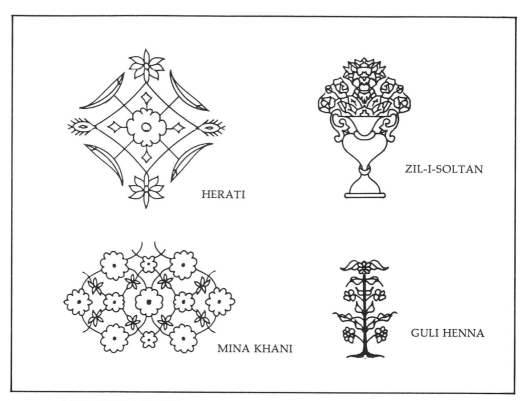

FIGURE 4: *REPEATED MOTIFS*

ZIL-I-SOLTAN

The Zil-i-soltan design is made up of multiple rows of repeated motifs, each of which resembles a vase of roses. This design is found more frequently in Qum and Abadeh; however, it is not restricted to those areas (see Figure 4).

BOTEH

The Boteh (paisley) design contains multiple rows of repeated *botehs* (pine cones or pears). It is probably the most widespread pattern, found in Persian, Caucasian, and some Turkoman rugs. Botehs come in many different forms and shapes, some of which are illustrated in Plates 9–14.

GUL

The Gul (Persian for "flower") is a distinctive rectilinear emblem unique to each Turkoman tribe (see Chapter 6, Figure 20). These multiple identical *guls* are arranged in rows.

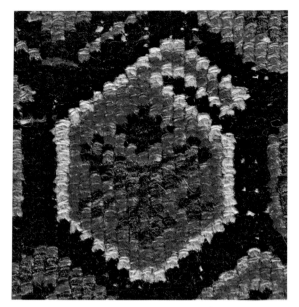

PLATE 9: *PERSIAN BOTEH (Shiraz)*

PLATE 10: *PERSIAN BOTEH (Tabriz)*

PLATE 11: *PERSIAN BOTEH (Senna)*   PLATE 12: *BALOUCH BOTEH*

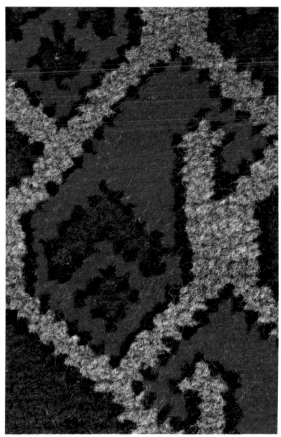

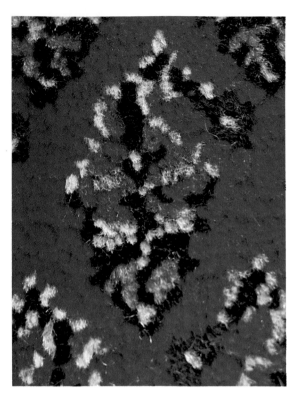

PLATE 13: *BOTEH (Seraband)*

PLATE 14: *CAUCASIAN BOTEH (Shirvan)*

PLATE 15: *GUL (Yomud)*

PLATE 16: *GARDEN DESIGN (Qum)*   PLATE 17: *SHAH ABBAS DESIGN (Qum)*

All-Over Design

The all-over design has a field filled with a pattern which has neither a "repeated" nor a regimented form. An all-over design will have very little repetition and a large-scale pattern which fills the field. In contrast, the "repeated" design fills the field with multiple rows of a single motif. Examples of the all-over designs are Shah Abbas, Garden (or Hunting), Tree (or Vase), Panel, and Picture (see Plates 16–19).

SHAH ABBAS

The Shah Abbas pattern (named for the patron of carpet-making, Shah Abbas the Great) is floral in character. The field is filled with palmettes and vases, which are interspersed within an intricate network of tendrils. The Shah Abbas pattern is woven often in Isfahan, Kashan, and Tabriz and occasionally in other carpet-weaving areas.

GARDEN OR HUNTING

The Garden or Hunting pattern represents a nature scene in which combinations of trees, flowers, animals, and birds, and human figures fill the field. The Hunting design is a variation of the Garden pattern, with the addition of hunters (usually with bow and arrow). The Garden pattern is woven in Qum as well as in other weaving centers; the Hunting pattern is most often associated with Tabriz.

TREE OR VASE

The Tree or Vase pattern contains a vase or tree centered at the base of the field from which emanate tendrils or branches; these, with flowers and leaves, fill the field. The Tree-of-life and the Weeping Willow (*Bid Majnūm*), examples of the tree pattern, are found in the carpets of Hamadan, and occasionally in those of Tabriz and Bijar. Vase patterns are woven most often in the carpets of Kashan.

PANEL DESIGN

Panel design carpets are easily recognized by the rectangular compart-

PLATE 18: *TREE OR VASE DESIGN (Isfahan)*   PLATE 19: *PANEL DESIGN (Tabriz)*

ments ("panels") into which the field is divided. Each compartment encloses one of a variety of motifs: flowers, trees, *boteh*, palmettes, and so on. The design was adopted from the matrix formed by irrigation channels in Persian gardens. Excellent examples of this design are woven in Tabriz and Qum.

PICTURE CARPETS

Picture carpets are those in which portraits or scenes are woven. Like a painting, picture carpets endeavor to realistically portray a specific person or place. They are rarely sold on the American market.

Prayer Rugs

Easily identifiable, the prayer rugs always have a prayer niche (*mihrab*) or arch present (see Plate 20). This arch may be geometric or curvilinear and the prayer niche either empty or filled with the various motifs common to the area in which the rug was woven (see Plate 51). Prayer rugs have been woven throughout Turkey, Iran, the Caucasus region, and Turkestan; copies of older prayer patterns are now being woven in Pakistan. A rug with multiple *mihrabs* is referred to as a *Saff* or a "family" prayer rug.

Borders

A series of borders or "frames" surround and set off the interior and major attraction of the carpet, its ground or field. Just as the field designs and motifs vary, the borders also differ. The standard arrangement is from three to seven borders, with a few exceptions. (Kerman, for example, weaves an Aubusson-type border; see Plate 59.) Borders are not limited to particular types of rugs, designs, or origin. Border designs have been freely borrowed, adopted, and adapted for each area's own use. (The Herati border used in the Herez rugs is stylized and geometric, as contrasted to the more intricate floral form of the Herati used in the rugs of Isfahan.) The number of borders varies from rug to rug, depending on its size, design, and origin. Generally, there is a single main border (*Ara-Khachi*), flanked by matching smaller borders (*Bala-Khachi*). The Bala-Khachi may be separated from the Ara-Khachi by lines or by even smaller minor borders.

Ara-Khachi that are widely used in Persian and on occasion in Turkish rugs are the Herati, a series of palmettes connected by flowering vines; cartouche, cloudlike enclosures containing poetic inscriptions or proverbs; *boteh*, which are interspersed with vines; and animal, or hunting, figures.

PANEL

SPANDREL

MIHRAB

FIELD

BORDER

PLATE 20:
*DESIGN AREAS
OF A PRAYER RUG*

In Caucasian and Turkish rugs the Ara-Khachi are more geometric, as in the stylized rosette, Kufic, and the serrated-leaf. (See Figure 5.)

Examples of Bala-Khachi found in Persian, Caucasian, and Turkish rugs are zig-zag, reciprocal, running dog, S-pattern, meandering vine and flower, and star (see Figure 6).

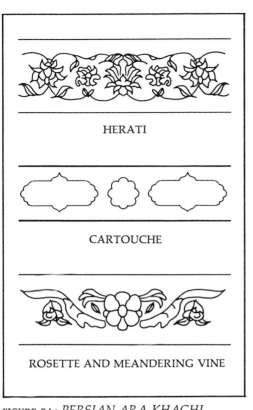

HERATI

CARTOUCHE

ROSETTE AND MEANDERING VINE

FIGURE 5A: *PERSIAN ARA-KHACHI*

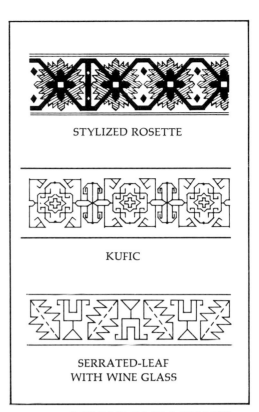

STYLIZED ROSETTE

KUFIC

SERRATED-LEAF
WITH WINE GLASS

FIGURE 5B: *CAUCASIAN ARA-KHACHI*

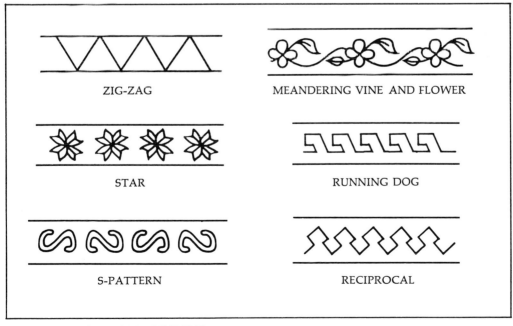

ZIG-ZAG

MEANDERING VINE AND FLOWER

STAR

RUNNING DOG

S-PATTERN

RECIPROCAL

FIGURE 6: *BALA-KHACHI DESIGNS*

Dates

Dates woven into Oriental rugs are not unusual. The numerals are in Persian script and can be easily translated to the more familiar western form (see Figure 7). Until recently the dates were based on the Mohammedan calendar, which starts with the Hegira, Mohammed's flight from Mecca on July 16, 622 A.D. Some Caucasian and Persian rugs were woven by Armenians who, being Christians, used the Gregorian calendar with Persian numerals. Based on the lunar year, the Mohammedan calendar is about one-third shorter than the solar year calendar used in Europe and the western hemisphere.

Converting the Persian numerals to the equivalent western date is complicated by several different dating practices. First, the lunar-based Moslem calendar is typically the basis for dates on antique and semi-antique rugs. Second, scattered instances of solar-based dates in Persian numerals—yet based on the Moslem calendar—have appeared since the early 1920s. Third, the Iranian calendar was changed in 1971 and is now dated from the founding of the Persian Empire 25 centuries ago; the calendar was also converted from the lunar to the solar year, with the New Year (*Now Ruz*) beginning on March 21. These dating practices complicate the conversion of Persian numerals to the equivalent western date.

CONVERSION PROCEDURES

To convert the *lunar-based Moslem date*, a simple mathematical procedure is necessary (see Figure 8). Converting the *solar-based Moslem date* requires only the addition of 622 to obtain its western equivalent.

To convert the current Iranian calendar dates, one must subtract 560 from the date. Occasionally, the Mohammedan date will have only three numbers, the first numeral (1) having been omitted. Woven dates have been known to have been altered; in such cases the second digit, usually a 3, is changed to a 2. This is more prevalent in Turkoman carpets than in the Persian or Caucasian carpets.

FIGURE 7: *NUMERICAL SIGNS*

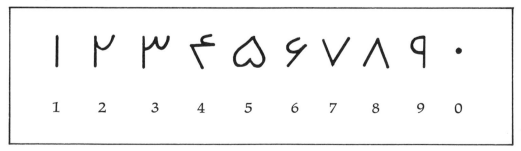

١ ٣ ٢ ٢	*convert to equivalent*		1322
	divide the date by 33		$1322 \div 33 = 40$
	subtract the quotient from the year		$1322 - 40 = 1282$
	add 622		$1282 + 622 = 1904$

FIGURE 8: *CONVERTING MOSLEM DATES*

A woven date can be helpful in establishing vintage. This might increase the asking price of an antique or semi-antique carpet because it eliminates some uncertainty regarding the rug's age. Dates woven into new carpets do not affect production costs or wholesale prices, and should not increase retail price.

Symbols and Myths

Over the years many different designs and motifs have been used in Oriental rugs. Some have had special symbolic significance attributed to them. The mystique of Oriental rugs owes a lot to the tales and fables that have been built up around the different design elements.

Even though designs, motifs, and colors have little or no particular significance today, there are traditional interpretations associated with them. Symbols and colors with deep religious meaning for one group or sect may have a completely different meaning for another. For example, a human or animal figure was rarely woven into a carpet made by Sunnite Moslems; they were very strict in their interpretation of the Koran law forbidding the use of figures that represent living creatures. By contrast, the Shi'ite Moslems freely used figures of humans and animals in their carpets.

The interpretations most often associated with the various colors and motifs are shown in Figures 9 and 10.

FIGURE 9: *TRADITIONAL COLOR INTERPRETATIONS*

COLOR	INTERPRETATION	COLOR	INTERPRETATION
RED	*Happiness, Joy*	BLACK	*Destruction*
BLUE	*Solitude, Truth*	ORANGE	*Devotion, Piety*
WHITE	*Purity, Peace, Grief*	YELLOW	*Power, Glory*
BROWN	*Fertility*	GREEN	*Paradise, "Prophet's Color," Sacred Color*

For the past hundred years, market demand has determined which designs and motifs have been woven. A nomadic or a seminomadic weaver would tend to weave either what she sees, translating it into characteristic formats, or what she has been taught. The village weaver, on the other hand, typically weaves what is ordered, according to the cartoon.

Each rug is a separate work of art and should be considered individually. Its value does not lie in the meaning of its motifs, but in the special feeling it arouses in the proud possessor.

FIGURE 10: *TRADITIONAL INTERPRETATION OF MOTIFS*

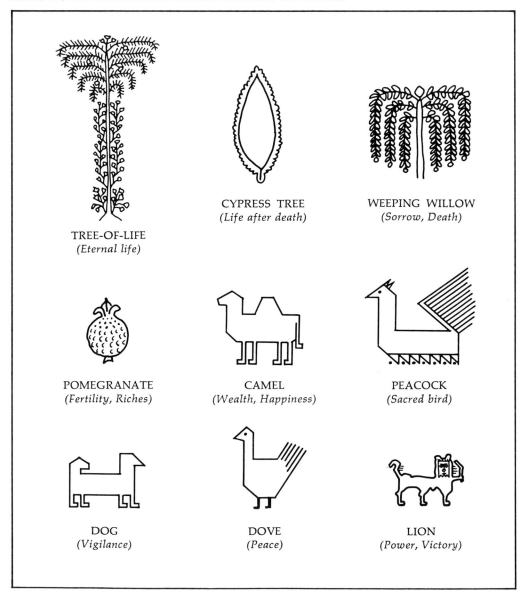

TREE-OF-LIFE
(*Eternal life*)

CYPRESS TREE
(*Life after death*)

WEEPING WILLOW
(*Sorrow, Death*)

POMEGRANATE
(*Fertility, Riches*)

CAMEL
(*Wealth, Happiness*)

PEACOCK
(*Sacred bird*)

DOG
(*Vigilance*)

DOVE
(*Peace*)

LION
(*Power, Victory*)

Persian (Iranian) Rugs

IRAN IS A COUNTRY rich in history and tradition which can be traced back over 2,500 years to the ancient Persian Empire. Known as Persia until 1935, Iran has for many centuries been noted for weaving the world's finest and most beautiful rugs.

Situated on a plateau in southwest Asia, Iran is almost completely surrounded by mountains. The land area is about two and a half times that of the state of Texas. For hundreds of years Iran was basically an agricultural nation; since the discovery of vast oil deposits in the early 1900s, however, the Pahlavi dynasty has transformed Iran into one of the world's more progressive nations. Iran's industrial and economic development has been especially dramatic under the present Shah, Mohammed Reza.

The majority of Iranians are of Aryan origin, part of the Indo-European race; 90 percent are Moslems. Many different ethnic groups also abide in Iran, including Kurds, Armenians, Arabs, and Balouchis, each maintaining its own heritage, traditions, and culture. These ethnic groups and tribes weave rugs that reflect the uniqueness and character of the weaver and his environs.

Even though the vast majority of Iranians are settled in towns and villages, some tribes still cling to the nomadic way of life. Carpets woven by nomads are generally labeled with the tribal name, such as Qashqai and Afshar; those made by settled (residing in a town or village) weavers are named for the town in which they are woven or where they were marketed, such as Kerman and Hamadan. Figure 11 shows the major weaving centers of Iran.

When translated into English, Iranian names often appear with several different spellings, a difficulty caused by the phonetic translation from Farsi (the modern Iranian language) to English. Alternate spellings are noted under specific rug headings.

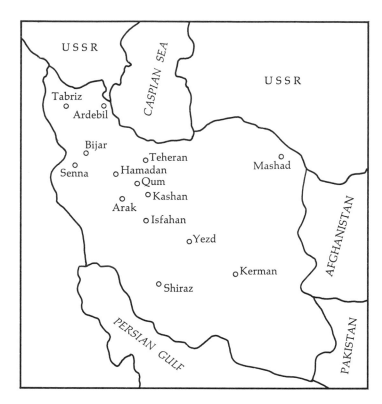

FIGURE 11: *MAJOR RUG-WEAVING CENTERS OF IRAN*

FIGURE 12: *AZERBAIJAN REGION*

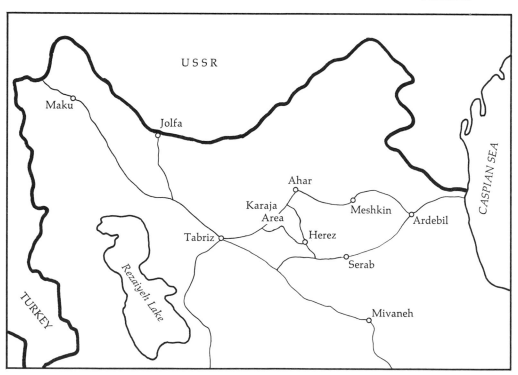

TABRIZ

KNOT: *Turkish*
WARP: *thick cotton*
WEFT: *cotton, double*
PILE: *coarse, heavy wool, cut short*
FRINGE: *plain or knotted at both ends*
SELVEDGE: *several warp threads overcast with wool*

It was in Tabriz that carpets were first woven strictly for export. In the mid-nineteenth century, the Tabrizi merchants collected and sent to Europe, via Istanbul, old and used carpets from homes and other sources. These carpets became so popular that demand soon exceeded the supply. Acknowledging the dwindling availability of rugs and foreseeing their eventual exhaustion, the enterprising Tabrizi merchants set up carpet-weaving houses or factories, to fulfill the demand.

The city of Tabriz is located in northwestern Iran, near the Russian and Turkish borders (see Figure 12). For centuries it has been a commercial center because of its location at the juncture of major trade routes to the Far East and southern Persia.

The weavers of Tabriz are among the most skilled in Iran. They use a hook that enables the weaver to tie a knot a second. The *Tabriz hook* (see Plate 6) consists of a knife, similar to that used in the other weaving centers, at the tip of which is a small hook. This unique implement enables the weaver to isolate a pair of warp threads, loop a strand of wool around the warps, then cut the strand free, all in one continuous motion.

Because of their attractive designs and colors, the carpets of Tabriz are the most popular Oriental rugs in the United States. Pastel colors such as ivory, pink, and blue, as well as the earth tones of brown, pistachio green, and rust, are commonly used. Red and navy blue are also used, but are not widely available on the American market.

A wide variety of well-executed designs are woven in Tabriz. The Hunting and Medallion designs are those most often encountered on the American market.

The Hunting design has become so strongly associated with the Tabriz that Hunting-design rugs woven in India and Rumania are called the Indian Tabriz and the Rumanian Tabriz. These rugs are generally not as well executed in either design or tightness of weave as their genuine Tabriz counterparts, and their much lower price reflects this.

The rugs of Tabriz are available in almost any size, from small mats and runners to the large gallery size. Round carpets are also woven in Tabriz.

PLATE 21: *TABRIZ (Medallion Design), 3 ft. 7 in. by 5 ft. 3 in.*
Courtesy of Capt. and Mrs. George Gipe

PLATE 22: *TABRIZ*
(Hunting Design)
2 ft. 8 in.
by 2 ft. 9 in.

PLATE 23: *TABRIZ*
(Medallion Design)
3 ft. diameter, round
Courtesy of Mr. and
Mrs. William Ennis

43

HEREZ *(Heriz)*

KNOT: *Turkish*
WARP: *cotton*
WEFT: *cotton, double, usually dyed light blue*
PILE: *medium; heavy, good-quality wool*
FRINGE: *plain or knotted fringe at both ends*
SELVEDGE: *overcast with wool*

The Herez area lies forty miles east of Tabriz, and consists of about thirty small villages, the more important of which are Herez, Ahar, Gorevan, and Meriban. The villages weave essentially the same design (see Plates 24 and 25), the only major difference being in quality: some Herez-area rugs are superior to others. Although the quality of weaving is not associated with specific villages, the names of the villages are used to denote the various grades of Herez-area rugs. The best of the Herez-area rugs is the *Herez;* those in the middle quality range are called *Meriban* or *Ahar.* The inferior grade, called *Gorevan,* was an excellent carpet at the turn of the century, but its quality began to deteriorate after World War I.

PLATE 24: *HEREZ*
3 ft. by 5 ft.
Courtesy of Mr. and
Mrs. George Sinkinson

44

Serapi is the name given by some rug dealers to older Herez-quality rugs. This labeling is incorrect and misleading. No village by that name exists in Iran, and the term is a corruption of Serab, a small village approximately halfway between Tabriz and Ardebil. Ninety percent of the rugs woven in Serab are runners, and show few similarities to the rugs of Herez in size or design.

Herez-area rugs are imported under their correct quality classification. When retailed, however, these rugs are often lumped together under the single label of "Herez."

Herez rugs are similar to those of Tabriz in design, both Herez and Tabriz weavers using the same medallion-and-corner cartoons. In Herez rugs the design is interpreted in a rectilinear fashion; in Tabriz, in a curvilinear fashion. Although they are more coarsely woven than the rugs of Tabriz, Herez rugs are very durable and will take heavy traffic. Most of the rugs were woven in the 8 by 10 feet to 10 by 14 feet sizes; however, smaller rugs are occasionally found.

KARAJA *(Karadja)*

KNOT:	*Turkish*
WARP:	*cotton*
WEFT:	*cotton, single*
PILE:	*good-quality wool, medium long*
FRINGE:	*knotted at both ends*
SELVEDGE:	*several warp threads overcast with cotton or wool*

The rugs of Karaja are woven in the small town of Karaja and in several smaller surrounding villages.

Their distinctive geometric design of three medallions makes the Karaja an easily identifiable rug (see Plate 26). The center medallion is dark blue, and the other two either cream or green. The field is usually madder red with a navy-blue main border; however, these colors are often reversed. Runners and the larger rugs have the same medallion motifs, but are sequenced to fill the field.

Most of the rugs woven are either smaller sizes or runners. Large sizes are made, but room-size rugs are rather uncommon.

PLATE 26: *KARAJA*
1 ft. 9 in. by 2 ft. 8 in.

ARDEBIL *(Ardabil)*

KNOT: *Turkish*
WARP: *cotton (wool in older rugs)*
WEFT: *cotton (wool in older rugs)*
PILE: *good-quality wool, cut short*
FRINGE: *knotted at both ends*
SELVEDGE: *several warp threads overcast with wool (cotton in newer rugs)*

Carpets woven in Ardebil, which is located just twenty miles south of the southernmost reaches of the Caucasus region, reflect a strong Caucasian influence (see Plates 27 and 28). A design with three notched, diamond-shaped medallions is most often used. The field may be filled with a variety of small geometric motifs and shapes: stars, rosettes, and human and animal figures. Other designs resemble those of the older Shirvans and Kabistans. A wide range of colors are used; cream, rust, and green are commonly used in the field, although reds, blues, and yellows are also found. The Ardebils are finely woven with good-quality wool. Since the 1950s more and more Ardebils have been appearing on the western market.

PLATE 27: *ARDEBIL*
4 ft. 6 in. by 7 ft. 3 in.
Courtesy of Mr. and Mrs. William Ennis

opposite,
PLATE 28: *ARDEBIL*
3 ft. by 4 ft. 8 in.
Courtesy of Mr. and
Mrs. Russell Summers

PLATE 29: *MESHKIN*
5 ft. 4 in. by 8 ft. 2 in.
Courtesy of Mr. and
Mrs. Richard LeNoir

MESHKIN

KNOT:	*Turkish*
WARP:	*wool or cotton*
WEFT:	*wool or cotton*
PILE:	*medium to medium long*
FRINGE:	*knotted at both ends*
SELVEDGE:	*overcast with wool*

Meshkin is about fifty miles northwest of Ardebil, just south of the Caucasus border. The designs of Meshkin, like those of Ardebil, resemble those of the older Caucasian rugs, and the bold geometric medallions used are similar to those of Kazak (see Plate 29). The colors used are more muted than the Ardebils, blues and earth tones of gold and brown. In addition, the weave is much coarser and the pile longer than that of Ardebil. All sizes are woven, from mats to room-sizes.

TRIBAL RUGS OF KURDISTAN *(Kurds)*

KNOT:	*Turkish*
WARP:	*wool or cotton*
WEFT:	*wool, double*
PILE:	*good-quality wool, medium long*
FRINGE:	*knotted at both ends*
SELVEDGE:	*several warp threads overcast with brown wool*

Kurdistan lies in what is now northwestern Iran, northern Iraq, southeastern Turkey, and the extreme northern tip of Syria. Kurdish tribes are not restricted to the loose boundaries of the Kurdistan region, but are widely scattered throughout western Iran and parts of Iraq, Turkey, and the Russian Caucasus (see Figure 13). Kurdish tribes are urbanized as well as nomadic or seminomadic. Rugs made by the nomadic and seminomadic tribes are referred to as Kurdish tribal rugs and are classed differently from the urban Kurdish tribes of Bijar and Senna.

Because characteristics of Kurdish tribal rugs vary according to the location of each tribe, individual rugs are often hard to identify. A strong Caucasian influence is evident among the northern Kurds; Anatolian elements are noticeable in the rugs of the western tribes. As a further complication in identification, the rugs may have a cotton warp and weft, a wool warp and weft, or a cotton warp and a wool weft. The pile is a heavy, good-quality wool. The weavers of the Jaffi tribe have a unique way of knotting their rugs, staggering knots so that they tie on the same pair of warp threads only in every second row of knots.*

The Herati, Mina Khani, and the Boteh are common designs used by the Kurdish tribes; however, designs vary among the tribes as often as do the weaving characteristics. (See Plate 30.)

---

* Murray Eiland, *Oriental Rugs: A Comprehensive Guide* (Greenwich, Conn.: New York Graphic Society, Ltd., 1973), p. 49.

PLATE 30: *KURD*
4 ft. by 6 ft.

SENNA *(Sehna, Senna, Sena)*

KNOT: *Turkish*
WARP: *cotton*
WEFT: *cotton, single*
PILE: *cut short*
FRINGE: *plain or knotted at both ends*
SELVEDGE: *several warp threads overcast with wool*

For several hundred years some of the finest Persian rugs have been woven in Senna (officially known as Sanandaj). The designs have changed very little over the years; the Herati pattern with a diamond-shaped medallion and the Boteh design are most often used. A repeated flower design (Gul-i-Mirza Ali or Guli Frank) indicates a definite French influence. (See Plate 31.)

Senna is the capital of the Iranian province of Kurdistan, a mountainous region in western Iran. The majority of the inhabitants of Senna, as well as most of the weavers, are Kurds of the Gurani tribe. These Kurds weave the closely knotted Senna rug only in the city; in the surrounding villages they weave the loosely knotted Kurdish tribal rugs.

The rugs of Senna are finely woven with good-quality wool. The warp in older rugs is often silk, in contrast to the cotton warp found in newer rugs. The Turkish knot is the only kind used in Senna rugs.

One of the finest Kelims is woven in Senna and the surrounding area. (See Chapter 8.)

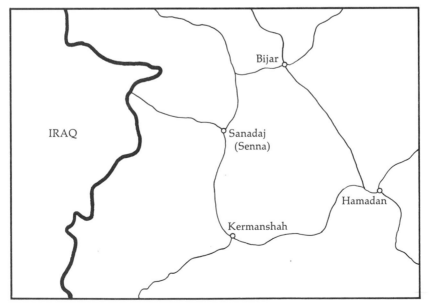

FIGURE 13:
*KURDISTAN
REGION*

opposite,
PLATE 31: *SENNA
4 ft. by 6 ft.
Courtesy of Mrs.
Burch Thomas*

BIJAR

KNOT:	*Turkish*
WARP:	*cotton (wool in older rugs)*
WEFT:	*cotton, wool, or both, triple*
PILE:	*cut short*
FRINGE:	kelim *at one end with knotted fringe at the other*
SELVEDGE:	*several warp threads overcast with wool*

The small town of Bijar is about forty miles northeast of Senna. The Bijar rugs are woven not only in Bijar, but also in a multitude of surrounding small villages.

Bijars are thick, tightly woven rugs with alternating warps depressed into the body of the rug. A unique feature of the wefts are the two thin cotton or wool wefts on either side of a thick wool weft thread. In weaving, the wefts are beaten down so firmly with a special comb used only in Bijar that the rug is quite stiff. The compactness of the fabric makes the carpet very sturdy.

The Herati pattern (with or without rectilinear medallion), Shah Abbas,

PLATE 32: *BIJAR*
2 ft. 2 in. by 3 ft.

and the Harshang (crab) designs are often used in the Bijar rugs in beautiful shades of dark blue, cherry red, and green (see Plates 32 and 33). Particularly intriguing is the Bijar sampler, in which various designs are illustrated by their incorporation into a single rug. In this way the weaving skills, as well as the individual designs, are passed on to future generations.

PLATE 33:
BIJAR SAMPLER
4 ft. by 6 ft.
Courtesy of Mr. and
Mrs. Tom Vance

HAMADAN

KNOT: *Turkish*
WARP: *cotton*
WEFT: *cotton, single*
PILE: *medium, good-quality wool*
FRINGE: kelim *at one end with plain fringe at the other*
SELVEDGE: *double overcast with wool*

Of all the rug-weaving centers in Iran, the Hamadan area is the largest in area as well as volume of rugs produced. The area is made up of hundreds of small towns and villages within a fifty-mile radius of the city of Hamadan (see Figure 14). The rugs of the more important of these small towns are marketed under their own name (*i.e.*, Bibikabad, Ingeles, and Dergazine). Since most of the rugs from the smaller, less important villages are marketed in the city of Hamadan, they are labeled as Hamadans, even though rugs made by each village possess their own identifiable characteristics.

The designs used in the Hamadan rugs are generally rectilinear; rod medallions and the Herati pattern are most often used (see Plates 34 and 35). During the 1920s and 1930s, many Hamadans were washed and painted. The weave varies from coarse to medium, the older Hamadans having a tighter weave. Excellent-quality wool is used, which makes the rugs wear exceptionally well.

Many Hamadans are available, both new and semi-antique. Although virtually all sizes are woven, the small sizes (3 by 5 to 4 by 6 feet) are most common.

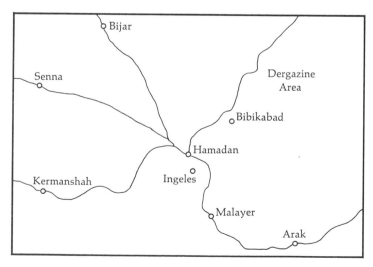

FIGURE 14:
HAMADAN AREA

opposite,
PLATE 34: *HAMADAN (Semi-Antique)*
3 ft. 4 in. by 5 ft. 3 in.
Courtesy of Mr. and Mrs. Russell Summers

PLATE 35: *HAMADAN, 3 ft. 4 in. by 4 ft. 11 in. Courtesy of Mr. Russell Herbert*

DERGAZINE *(Dergezine, Dargazin)*

KNOT:	*Turkish*
WARP:	*cotton*
WEFT:	*cotton, single*
PILE:	*medium, excellent-quality wool*
FRINGE:	kelim *at one end with knotted fringe at the other*
SELVEDGE:	*double overcast with wool*

If for no other reason, Dergazine is important for the volume of rugs produced over the years. The wealthiest district of the Hamadan area, the artisans of Dergazine have been weaving rugs for over four hundred years.* Some sixty small villages make up the Dergazine district, which is fifty miles northeast of Hamadan.

All Dergazines are similar in design, and have been strongly influenced by the Sarouk; both use a field filled with detached floral sprays. The ground colors are either red or navy blue. (See Plates 36 and 37.) During the 1920s and 1930s Dergazines, like the Sarouks, were washed and painted. The majority of Dergazine rugs are runners, although small rugs and mats are also woven. These rugs are extremely durable.

---

* A. Cecil Edwards, *The Persian Carpet* (London: Duckworth, 1975), p. 91.

PLATE 36: *DERGAZINE*
3 ft. 6 in. by 5 ft. 2 in.
Courtesy of Mr. and Mrs. Richard LeNoir

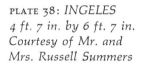

opposite,
PLATE 37: *DERGAZINE*
3 ft. 4 in. by 5 ft. 2 in.
Courtesy of Mr. and
Mrs. Paul Roberts

PLATE 38: *INGELES*
4 ft. 7 in. by 6 ft. 7 in.
Courtesy of Mr. and
Mrs. Russell Summers

INGELES *(Ingelas, Injilas, Angelas)*

KNOT:	*Turkish*
WARP:	*cotton*
WEFT:	*cotton, single*
PILE:	*medium to medium long in length, excellent-quality wool*
FRINGE:	kelim *at one end with plain fringe at the other*
SELVEDGE:	*double overcast with wool*

Ingeles, a small village south of Hamadan, produces one of the best-quality rugs made in the Hamadan district. Only two designs are used, the Herati and the Mir-i-boteh. These can be woven either with or without a center medallion. The ground color is a cherry red with borders of navy and white. (See Plate 38.) Most of the rug production of Ingeles is in small sizes (3 by 5 to 4 by 6 feet) or runners.

BIBIKABAD

KNOT:	*Turkish*
WARP:	*cotton*
WEFT:	*cotton, single, occasionally dyed blue*
PILE:	*medium long, heavy good-quality wool*
FRINGE:	*plain fringe at both ends*
SELVEDGE:	*overcast with wool*

The rugs labeled as Bibikabad are made in the small villages of Bibikabad and Ainabad, which lie approximately thirty miles northeast of Hamadan. The Herati and the Mir-i-boteh are the only designs woven, and appear either with or without a center medallion. The colors are navy blue, madder red, and ivory. (See Plate 39.) Bibikabads are woven in larger sizes (9 by 12 to 10 by 17 feet); smaller rugs are uncommon. These carpets are loosely woven with good-quality wool, making them ideal for heavy traffic areas. The *jufti,* or false knot (see page 22), has appeared in recent rugs, so caution should be used when buying them.

PLATE 39: *BIBIKABAD 4 ft. 2 in. by 4 ft. 8 in. Courtesy of Mr. and Mrs. Jack Florin*

SAROUK AND THE ARAK WEAVING AREA *(Saruk)*

KNOT:	*Persian*
WARP:	*cotton*
WEFT:	*cotton, double, usually dyed blue*
PILE:	*short, good-quality wool, tightly woven*
FRINGE:	kelim *at one end with knotted fringe at the other, or knotted fringe at both ends*
SELVEDGE:	*double overcast with wool the same color as the ground*

Sarouk rugs are woven not only in Sarouk but in Arak and many of the small surrounding-area villages (see Figure 15). Thousands of Sarouks were imported to the United States from the turn of the century until 1960, at which time they were diverted to fill the surging demand of the European market. The Sarouks that were made for the U.S. market varied little in design, having a floral field filled with detached floral sprays and a central floral-bouquet motif. The ground color was rose red to maroon, and nearly all the rugs were washed and painted. The main border was a navy blue Herati border pattern. These tightly woven rugs were made in all sizes from the smallest mats to large gallery sizes (1 by 2 to 15 by 30 feet).

The newer Sarouks, most of which find their way to the European market, have a medallion-and-corner design or use the Shah Abbas pattern. Ivory is often used as a ground color.

FIGURE 15: *ARAK WEAVING AREA*

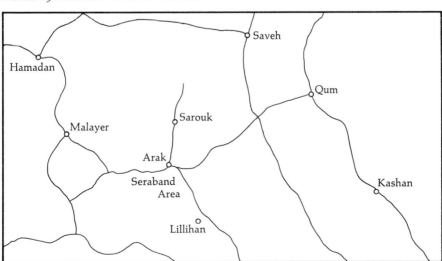

Other rugs from the same area are woven with the detached floral spray "Sarouk" pattern. (See Plate 40.) The difference between these rugs and the Sarouks is the tightness of weave. While these rugs may be identical to the Sarouk in pattern, they are not Sarouks; in order of decreasing quality they are labeled Arak, Sultanabad, Mahal, and Mushkabad. The latter two are inferior bazaar-quality carpets often woven with "skin" or dead wool and inferior dyes.

PLATE 40: *SAROUK*
3 ft. 3 in. by 5 ft. 2 in.
Courtesy of Mr. and
Mrs. Donald Dieterich

ARAK / SULTANABAD

KNOT:	*Persian*
WARP:	*cotton*
WEFT:	*cotton, double, dyed blue*
PILE:	*medium to medium long, good-quality wool*
FRINGE:	*kelim at one end with knotted fringe at the other, or knotted fringe at both ends*
SELVEDGE:	*double overcast with wool the same color as the ground*

Arak and Sultanabad rugs are woven in the west-central Iranian town of Arak (once called Sultanabad) as well as in the surrounding area. Though rugs labeled as Araks and Sultanabads are made in the same town or area, they are different rugs, although the variation is only in tightness of weave. As mentioned in the section under Sarouk, the Arak is a slightly higher quality rug than the Sultanabad. These generalizations also apply to the non-Sarouk patterns woven in the Arak area. The Herati, Shah Abbas, and the medallion designs are all used frequently in and around Arak. Common ground colors are red, blue, and ivory. The larger sizes are more often woven, especially in the 8 by 10 to 9 by 12 feet sizes. Though these rugs are not as tightly woven as Sarouks, they are made with good-quality wool and wear extremely well.

LILLIHAN *(Lilihan)*

KNOT:	*Persian*
WARP:	*cotton*
WEFT:	*cotton, single*
PILE:	*medium short in length*
FRINGE:	*kelim at one end with plain fringe at the other*
SELVEDGE:	*double overcast with blue wool*

Twenty-five miles south of Arak lies the small town of Lillihan. Rugs were produced here that were very similar to the Sarouk in design, but resemble the Hamadan in weave. Lillihans are easily recognized by their rose-pink or rose-red ground, and by the blue and azure colors used in the motifs and borders. The typical design is an overall floral pattern in which floral sprays surround a central floral-bouquet medallion. (See Plates 41 and 42.) As with the Sarouks of the 1920s and 1930s, most of the Lillihans were chemically washed and then painted.

Very few Lillihans are being woven today; most of the town's weaving has been diverted to producing Sarouks. Many semi-antique Lillihans may be found, however, especially in the smaller (3 by 5 to 4 by 6 feet) sizes.

PLATE 41: *LILLIHAN (Antique), 4 ft. by 7 ft. Courtesy of Mr. and Mrs. Clair Harrah*

PLATE 42: *LILLIHAN, 3 ft. 3 in. by 4 ft. 6 in.*

SERABAND

KNOT:	*Turkish, occasionally Persian*
WARP:	*cotton*
WEFT:	*cotton, often dyed blue; double*
PILE:	*medium, thick heavy wool*
FRINGE:	kelim *at one end with plain or knotted fringe at the other*
SELVEDGE:	*double overcast with wool*

Seraband rugs are made in the Sarawan district, about twenty miles south-west of Arak. Despite the proximity to Arak, Seraband rugs are far more closely related to the rugs of Hamadan. Rugs have been woven in this area for several hundred years.

The antique Seraband, called the Mir-Seraband, is a quite different rug from those produced in the area today. Since they have not been woven since the turn of the century, Mir-Serabands are rare today. With a tighter weave and of much finer quality than its loosely woven present-day counterpart, Mir-Serabands were usually woven in the Mir-i-boteh pattern, although the Herati design was occasionally used. The present-day Seraband always has the Mir-i-boteh design, and the main border continues to be ivory with the *Schekeri* design (a continuous vine with *boteh*). The ground color is either red or dark blue. (See Plate 43.) The Mir-Serabands were woven in small sizes or *kelleis* (5 by 15 feet); the modern Serabands are found in sizes ranging from small to 8 by 10 feet.

Not all Mir-i-boteh rugs are Serabands. The Arak area weaves a tightly knotted rug called the Seraband-Sarouk; these excellent-quality rugs resemble the Sarouk in weave and usually come in 4 by 6 to 9 by 12 feet sizes.

PLATE 43: *SERABAND (Portion)*
7 ft. by 10 ft.
Courtesy of Mr. and Mrs. Porter Godard

MALAYER

KNOT:	*Turkish, Persian*
WARP:	*cotton*
WEFT:	*cotton; single or double*
PILE:	*medium*
FRINGE:	*kelim at one end with knotted fringe at the other*
SELVEDGE:	*double overcast with blue wool*

Halfway between Hamadan and Arak are the approximately 120 villages of the Malayer district that surround the town of Malayer. The villages northwest of Malayer, toward Hamadan, produce a carpet very similar to the Hamadan in weave. (See Plate 44.) The villages southeast of Malayer, toward Arak, weave a fine-quality carpet very similar in weave to the Sarouk. Commonly called Malayer Sarouks, these rugs are Turkish-knotted, a feature that at times provides the only clue in distinguishing them from a Sarouk. Rugs produced in Josan, the most important of these minor villages, are known on the rug market as Josan Sarouks.

PLATE 44: *MALAYER (Hamadan)*
2 ft. by 3 ft.
Courtesy of Mr. and
Mrs. George Sinkinson

FERAHAN

KNOT: *Persian*
WARP: *cotton*
WEFT: *cotton, double*
PILE: *short, finely knotted*
FRINGE: kelim *at one end with knotted fringe at the other*
SELVEDGE: *overcast with wool*

The Ferahan district is located between Arak and Sarouk. Few, if any, Ferahan carpets have been made since the turn of the century. The weaving in this area is now limited to Sarouks, Araks, and the lower quality rugs of the Arak area.

The Herati pattern, with or without a medallion, was the most common design woven, although the Mina Khani and the Guli Henna were also used. Ferahans featured either a dark blue or red ground, with green often used in the motifs and the main border (see Plate 45). Most Ferahans were woven in small sizes. They have become difficult to obtain in recent times.

PLATE 45: *FERAHAN*
3 ft. by 5 ft.
Courtesy of Mr. John Campbell, Jr.

ISFAHAN *(Ispahan, Esfahan)*

KNOT:	*Persian*
WARP:	*cotton or silk*
WEFT:	*cotton, double*
PILE:	*short, good- to excellent-grade wool*
FRINGE:	*narrow* kelim *with plain fringe at both ends*
SELVEDGE:	*double overcast with wool*

Isfahan is regarded as one of the most beautiful cities in the world. Carpet-weaving here can be traced back to the sixteenth century, when Isfahan was the capital of Persia under Shah Abbas. The weaving looms were destroyed in the Afghan invasion of 1722, and little weaving was done until the carpet industry had its rebirth in the early 1920s. Most of these carpets were then exported to Europe. These rugs were woven with inferior wool; their colors were too bright and their pile too short, and they were not popular in Europe. After World War II, the quality greatly improved, and many of the rugs were produced for the home market.

Overall, the Isfahan is one of the finest rugs woven in Iran today. At its best the Isfahan is unsurpassed in quality.

The designs of Isfahan and Nain are very similar; the Shah Abbas and the medallion-and-corner (see Plate 46) are the two most commonly woven designs, although the Tree-of-life and prayer designs are also used in Isfahan. In the field, an ivory or pastel blue are the most frequently used colors; red grounds are also woven.

Isfahans have never been imported in great quantities to the U.S. market. Although a variety of sizes are available, the most common sizes found are 4 by 7 to 8 by 10 feet.

PLATE 46: *ISFAHAN, 4 ft. by 6 ft.*
Courtesy of Mr. and Mrs. F.A. Brubaker

NAIN

KNOT: *Persian*
WARP: *cotton or silk*
WEFT: *cotton or silk, double*
PILE: *short, excellent-quality wool*
FRINGE: *knotted at both ends*
SELVEDGE: *double overcast with wool*

Sixty miles east of Isfahan lies the small town of Nain, the carpet-makers of which produce one of the finest carpets in Iran. Nain artisans began weaving rugs only in the early 1930s, after having been renowned for centuries for the fine woolen cloth made there. When the import of western fabrics and fashions brought about the decline of the cloth-weaving industry, craftsmen undertook the weaving of carpets in the same tradition of excellence. Their weave is comparable in knot count to the best of the antique carpets.

Nain designs are very similar to those of Isfahan. The Shah Abbas (with an ivory ground) and the medallion designs (with blue or, more rarely, red ground) are woven most often (see Plate 47). Silk may be used in the Nain to outline many of the motifs; all-silk rugs are also made. Measured against the total volume of rugs made in Nain, very few Nains are exported to the United States. The rugs are quite expensive, and those that are imported are usually in the smaller sizes (4 by 6 feet or smaller).

However fine the knot count, Nain rugs lack variety in the designs and colors used.

PLATE 47: *NAIN, 3 ft. by 5 ft. Courtesy of Mr. and Mrs. William Campbell, Jr.*

74

PLATE 48: *NAIN (Garden Design), 2 ft. by 4 ft.*
Courtesy of Mr. and Mrs. Seymour Walker

QUM *(Ghoum, Qom)*

KNOT: *Persian*
WARP: *cotton or silk*
WEFT: *cotton or silk*
PILE: *short, excellent-quality wool*
FRINGE: *knotted at both ends*
SELVEDGE: *double overcast with wool*

Qum, ninety miles south of Tehran, is one of the holiest cities in Iran; Mohammed's daughter Fatima is buried here. The weaving industry of Qum was begun in the early 1930s by merchants from Kashan.

A wide variety of designs are used in Qum: the Panel design, Garden design, Zil-i-soltan (vase of roses), Boteh, prayer, and Shah Abbas. All are beautifully and skillfully executed, with a wide array of colors used in the motifs and grounds (see Plates 49 and 50). Not only are beautiful all-silk rugs woven, but silk is often woven into wool rugs to outline and accent the motifs. A Qum is regarded as one of the finest rugs made today and, as one might expect, its quality is reflected in its price. Small sizes are most common.

PLATE 49: *QUM (Garden Design)*
3 ft. 2 in. by 5 ft.
Courtesy of Mr. and Mrs. Russell Summers

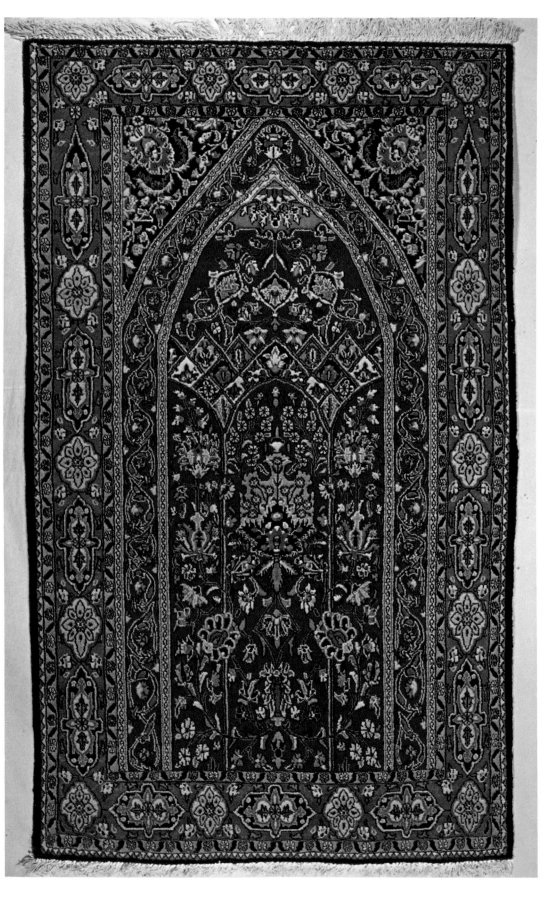

opposite,
PLATE 50: *QUM (Prayer Design)*
3 ft. 5 in. by 5 ft. 8 in.

PLATE 51: *KASHAN (Prayer Design)*
3 ft. 8 in. by 5 ft. 2 in
Courtesy of Dr. and Mrs. John Campbell

KASHAN

KNOT:	*Persian*
WARP:	*cotton*
WEFT:	*cotton, double*
PILE:	*short, excellent quality*
FRINGE:	*knotted at both ends*
SELVEDGE:	*double overcast with wool*

Kashan is located in central Iran about 150 miles south of Tehran. The carpet-weaving industry of Kashan, like that of Isfahan, was destroyed when the Afghans invaded Persia in 1722. Since weaving was begun again in the late nineteenth century, Kashan has established and maintained a reputation for making one of the finest Persian rugs.

The traditional designs woven in Kashan are the Shah Abbas and the medallion-and-corner, with a red ground. More recently, Kashan has adopted the Garden design with an ivory ground, although the traditional designs are still woven. Kashan is noted also for its prayer rugs, which artisans weave in either wool or silk (see Plate 51).

JOSHAGHAN

KNOT:	*Persian*
WARP:	*cotton*
WEFT:	*cotton, double usually dyed blue*
PILE:	*heavy, good-quality wool, short to medium in length*
FRINGE:	*small* kelim *with plain fringe at both ends*
SELVEDGE:	*double overcast with blue wool*

Rugs have been woven in the central Iranian village of Joshaghan for several hundred years. Designs have changed very little, and are restricted to a few variations of the medallion-and-corner pattern. Separate Guli Henna, Mina Khani, and Bid Majnūm (Weeping Willow) motifs are clustered in diamond shapes scattered throughout the field, and a diamond-shaped medallion, often outlined in white, is sometimes present. The ground color is usually madder red, with blue and white used in the motifs. (See Plate 52.)

The wool comes from the sheep of surrounding mountain area and is of excellent quality.

PLATE 52: *JOSHAGHAN*
3 ft. 6 in. by 5 ft. 4 in.

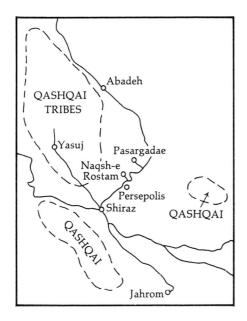

PLATE 53: *SHIRAZ*
4 ft. by 6 ft.

SHIRAZ

KNOT:	*Persian*
WARP:	*wool; dark brown or natural, or a mixture of both*
WEFT:	*wool; double; dark brown, natural or dyed red*
PILE:	*medium to medium long*
FRINGE:	*wide* kelim *(often striped) with plain fringe*
SELVEDGE:	*overcast with alternating colored wool*

Rugs that are commonly called Shiraz are woven by many different nomadic and seminomadic tribes of the Fars region (see Figure 16). These rugs derive their name from the fact that they are marketed in Shiraz, the provincial capital.

Small Persian villages scattered around Shiraz and a loosely organized federation of many unrelated Arab, Turkish, and Luri tribes are the largest

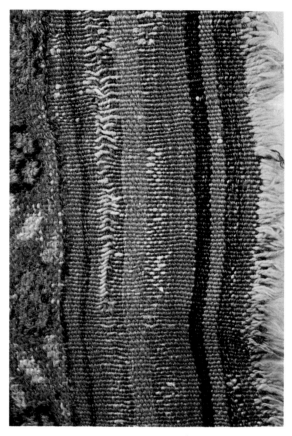

PLATE 54: *SHIRAZ, 3 ft. by 5 ft.*

PLATE 55: *DETAIL OF KELIM, showing the characteristic banding of the Shiraz.*

and most important sources of rugs in the province—about 80 percent of the province's total rug output. Each of the villages produces rugs generally indistinguishable in quality and design from those of the other villages and are grouped and labeled as Shiraz, rather than by their tribal or village origin. These village-area rugs usually have a Persian knot and a single woolen weft thread. The rugs woven by the federation may either be made with a Persian or a Turkish knot or a double- or a single-weft thread, depending on the individual tribe.

The differences between the rugs of the Persian Villagers and those of the recently settled nomadic tribes are often hazy. There is often intermarriage between the villagers and the nomads of the same plain or valley. It is quite difficult in such cases to determine the origin of a rug from that area.

The rugs of Shiraz have geometric designs; a rectilinear pole medallion, as well as many other geometric designs, are used. The selvedges in the older Shiraz rugs have a barber-pole effect, with two or more alternating bands of colors; however, the barber-pole effect may not always be found in newer rugs. (See Plates 53 through 55.)

QASHQAI *(Kashgai, Ghasqai)*

KNOT: *Turkish*
WARP: *wool*
WEFT: *wool, double*
PILE: *medium, thick, excellent-quality wool*
FRINGE: kelim *with plain or knotted fringe at both ends*
SELVEDGE: *overcast with alternating colors of wool*

The Qashqai are the best weavers and the most prosperous of all of the tribes of Fars. Women do all of the weaving and take great pride in their rugs. The wool, which comes from Qashqai sheep, is washed, spun, and dyed with great care. It is soft and develops a beautiful patina.

Designs are typically geometric, consisting of a Tree-of-life or a diamond-shaped medallion or medallions. Small stylized figures and other small geometric motifs are scattered throughout the field. (See Plate 56.)

Most of the Qashqai weaving is in small rugs, saddle bags, or tent bags. The excellence of the Qashqai rugs is reflected in their price; they are more expensive than most nomadic or seminomadic rugs.

PLATE 56: *QASHQAI, 3 ft. by 5 ft. Courtesy of Dr. and Mrs. L.A. Graham*

83

PLATE 57: *YELEMEH*
3 ft. 5 in. by 5 ft. 2 in.

YELEMEH

KNOT:	*Persian or Turkish*
WARP:	*wool*
WEFT:	*dark-brown wool; single or double*
PILE:	*soft, good-quality; medium length*
FRINGE:	*knotted at both ends*
SELVEDGE:	*two colors alternating in diagonal stripes*

Yelemeh rugs are relatively new to the western market, having been made only since World War II. These rugs are produced by both the Persian Villagers and the Qashqai in the area between Shiraz and Abadeh. They are rectilinear in design, with latch-hooked diamond-shaped medallions; small geometric motifs are found throughout the field. The newer rugs have beautiful shades of green, yellow, orange, red, and blue, whereas the older rugs have more red, blue, and beige (see Plate 57).

The Yelemehs may be woven with the Persian or Turkish knot, depending on whether they are made by the Persian Villagers or the Qashqai. The warp and weft are usually wool, with a dark brown weft thread, although in the village rugs cotton may be used. The pile is a soft, good-quality wool.

ABADEH

KNOT: *Persian*

WARP: *cotton*

WEFT: *cotton, dyed light blue, double*

PILE: *short, good-quality wool*

FRINGE: *narrow* kelim *with either plain or knotted fringe at both ends*

SELVEDGE: *double overcast with wool*

Abadeh, located approximately halfway between Isfahan and Shiraz, has been producing carpets for export for only the past thirty years. Most of the designs woven have been borrowed from other weaving areas. The diamond medallion pattern with corner rosettes (see Plate 58) is an adaptation of a Qashqai tribal pattern. The Zil-i-soltan, or vase of roses, design is also a common design woven in Abadeh.

The rugs of Abadeh are woven with good-quality wool and are recommended for their durability. The most common colors found in the Abadehs are red, cream, and blue.

PLATE 58: *ABADEH*
2 ft. 3 in. by 3 ft. 7 in.
Courtesy of Mr. and
Mrs. William Ennis

KERMAN

KNOT:	*Persian*
WARP:	*cotton*
WEFT:	*cotton, double*
PILE:	*medium length*
FRINGE:	*knotted fringe at both ends*
SELVEDGE:	*overcast with wool the same color as the ground*

The province of Kerman is an area in southeastern Iran; the city of Kerman is its provincial capital and main city. Kerman rugs are woven in the city as well as in many of the surrounding villages. Weaving in Kerman can be traced as far back as the seventeenth century, although the rug industry remained small scale until its overall expansion in the late nineteenth century.

The Kerman rugs have always been favorites on the western market. All Kermans are floral, but variations are made to suit the tastes of the three major markets of the United States, Europe, and Iran. The American Kerman is known for its pastel colors, central medallion, and either an open or a semi-open field (see Plate 59). The Iranian Kerman has a cochineal-red ground with a central medallion and an open field; it has a tighter weave and shorter pile than those imported to the United States. The European Kerman has small detached floral sprays with a central medallion and comes in pastel colors (see Plate 60). All sizes are woven, from the smallest mats to large gallery sizes.

LAVER KERMAN

Some of the finest antique Kerman rugs came from the small village of Ravar, which in the West is known as Laver. Today the rug-makers of Ravar weave Kermans indistinguishable from those made in the city of Kerman proper.

KERMANSHAH

The labeling of rugs as "Kermanshah" is controversial, since few disputed rugs were ever woven there. The town of Kermanshah is a Kurd tribal village 900 miles from Kerman, noted for its wool marketplace. Any rugs woven there are Kurds, and bear the definite characteristics of Kurdish rather than Kerman rugs.

The designation "Kermanshah" might lead one to believe that a rug bearing that name is a superior Kerman or Kerman-design rug. "Kermanshah" has been generally accepted as referring to design rather than origin, specifically, an intricate all-over floral pattern, either with or without a central medallion. No new rug should be referred to as a Kermanshah; if it was woven in the town of Kermanshah, it is a Kurd; if it displays Kerman characteristics, it is a Kerman.

PLATE 59:
KERMAN
(American Design)
5 ft. 2 in.
by 8 ft. 4 in.
Courtesy of
Mr. and Mrs.
Raymond Allen

opposite,
PLATE 60: KERMAN
(European Design)
4 ft. 8 in.
by 8 ft. 4 in.
Courtesy of
Mr. and Mrs.
William Ennis

PLATE 61: *AFSHAR (Morgi Design) signed Reza Khan*
2 ft. by 1 ft. Courtesy of Mr. and Mrs. John Griffis

AFSHAR

KNOT:	*Persian or Turkish*
WARP:	*cotton or wool*
WEFT:	*single cotton, double wool*
PILE:	*very good–quality wool, medium length*
FRINGE:	*knotted or plain fringe at both ends*
SELVEDGE:	*double overcast with blue wool*

Afshari rugs are made by nomads and villagers whose life-styles are very similar to those of the Qashqai and Persian Villagers of Fars. The Afshari area is to the south and southwest of the city of Kerman.

Afshari villagers weave their rugs with a Persian knot on a cotton foundation, while the nomads use a Turkish knot on a woolen foundation. The Afshari employ a variety of designs: large floral sprays borrowed from Kerman, repeated rows of large geometric *boteh*, diamond-shaped medallions similar to those of Shiraz, and the *Morgi* design. The Morgi ("hen") pattern (see Plate 61) is an imaginative design that originated with the Afshari, although it has since been adopted in the Fars region. A geometric motif, resembling a chicken, is repeated throughout the field. Afshari rugs are usually small, rarely over 5 by 7 feet. Vegetable dyes are still used; red, cream, and blue are common ground colors.

YEZD

KNOT: *Persian*
WARP: *cotton*
WEFT: *cotton, double, dyed blue*
PILE: *medium in length*
FRINGE: *narrow* kelim *at both ends with fringe*
SELVEDGE: *overcast with blue wool*

Carpets were woven in Yezd as early as the seventeenth century, but until recently the weaving was on a very small scale. Few of the Yezd carpets have been imported to the United States, although they are quite popular on the European and the Persian markets.

The Herati pattern and the medallion-and-corner design appear most often in Yezd rugs. The older Yezd carpets resemble the Tabriz in structure; the newer carpets are more similar to the Kermans. Usually large and room-size, these carpets are very durable. Red and blue are the most common ground colors, but bright colors such as yellows and creams are also found in the designs.

CARPETS OF KHURASAN *(Khurassan)*

Occupying most of the northeast quadrant of Iran is the huge province of Khurasan (see Figure 17). Northern Khurasan is one of the major wool-producing areas of Iran. Rugs from the Khurasan province fall into three major classifications: Khurasan, Mashad, and Birjand.

KHURASAN

No new carpets are being imported as Khurasans. Most authorities use the term to denote antique and semi-antique rugs with a Herati pattern, from the Khurasan province. These had a unique weft structure in which a single weft was passed between three or four rows of knots; then, three or four wefts were passed between the next two rows of knots, giving the back of the carpet a ribbed appearance. These rugs are extremely rare today.

MASHAD

Rugs that originate in the Mashad area need to be divided into two groups: the *Mashad* rugs, woven in the small towns and villages surrounding the town of Mashad, and the *Turkibaff*, which are woven in the city of Mashad proper.

The two kinds of rugs are similar in design; the Shah Abbas design, with or without a medallion, may be used with a dark cochineal-red field. The other common design is the Herati with medallion and corners, generally woven in several shades of blue and ivory. Both groups of rugs are usually woven in large, room sizes, 9 by 12 feet, or larger.

FIGURE 17: *RUG-WEAVING CENTERS OF EASTERN IRAN AND THE TRIBAL WEAVING AREAS OF THE BALOUCHI*

PLATE 62: *MASHAD (Portion) 10 ft. by 12 ft. Courtesy of Mr. and Mrs. Robert Smith*

The Mashads are tied with a Persian knot on four warp threads instead of the usual two. Because this has always been the case with Mashad rugs and is an accepted standard *in these rugs only,* they are not termed *jufti.* The pile is a soft, thick wool obtained from the fall shearing, which does not wear as well as that taken in the spring shearing. (See Plate 62.)

The Turkibaff carpets are woven with the Turkish knot on two warp threads. These rugs are a better quality than Mashads, and are generally woven with wool taken in the spring shearing.

MASHAD

KNOT:	*Persian*
WARP:	*cotton, knots tied on four warp threads*
WEFT:	*cotton*
PILE:	*medium, good-quality wool*
FRINGE:	*plain fringe at both ends*
SELVEDGE:	*double overcast with wool*

TURKIBAFF

KNOT:	*Turkish*
WARP:	*cotton, knots tied on two warp threads*
WEFT:	*cotton*
PILE:	*medium, excellent-quality wool*
FRINGE:	*plain fringe at both ends*
SELVEDGE:	*double overcast with wool*

MUD (Moute)

Another excellent quality rug of the Khurasan area is woven in the small village of Mud. The Mud is usually woven with a Herati pattern on an ivory ground. (See Plate 63.)

BIRJAND

The rugs labeled as Birjands now refer to the lowest grades of carpet woven in the Khurasan province. Comparable in quality to the Mahal rugs of the Arak area, Birjands are woven in the town of Birjand and in the surrounding area. The same designs used in Mashad are woven in Birjand, as is the practice of tying Persian knots around four warp threads.

PLATE 63: *MUD, 2 ft. 10 in. by 4 ft. 2 in.*
Courtesy of Mr. and Mrs. William Ennis

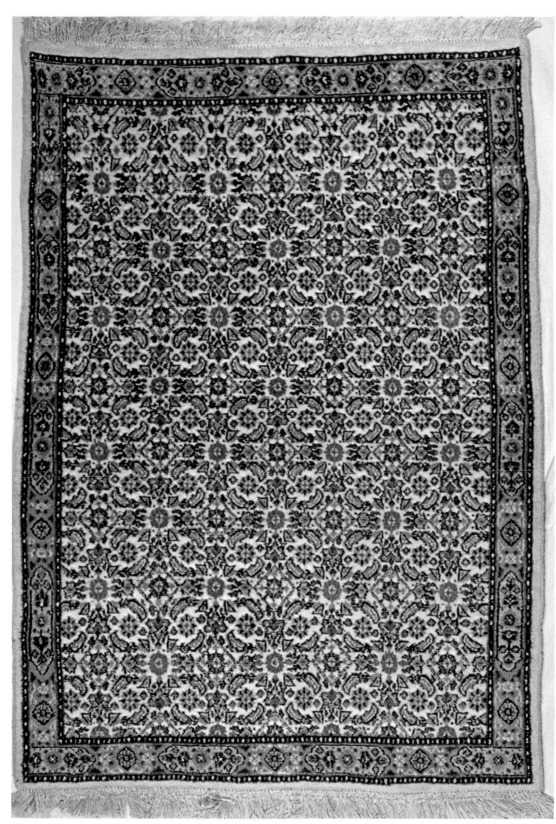

BALOUCHI *(Baluchi, Belouchi)*

KNOT:	*Persian*
WARP:	*wool or cotton (new rugs from Iran)*
WEFT:	*wool, usually dark colored*
PILE:	*short to medium (new rugs from Iran)*
FRINGE:	*wide kelim often decorated with small motifs or stripes*
SELVEDGE:	*double selvedge overcast with dark-colored goat's hair*

Contrary to what might be expected, Balouchi rugs are *not* woven in Balouchistan. They are made in the Khurasan province of northeast Iran, and in the west and southwest portion of Afghanistan, by Balouchi tribes and also by a few Arab tribes near Firdaus. In Iran the rugs woven by the Balouchi tribes are marketed in Mashad; those woven in Afghanistan are usually marketed in Herat.

Balouchi rugs resemble Turkoman rugs not only in color but also in some designs, which may vary depending on the rug's origin. The Arab tribes around Firdaus weave a rug which may employ either diagonal or vertical stripes. Turkoman-style (Tekke) *guls* may be woven by Balouchis living in northern areas near Turkoman tribes. Balouchi tribes are noted

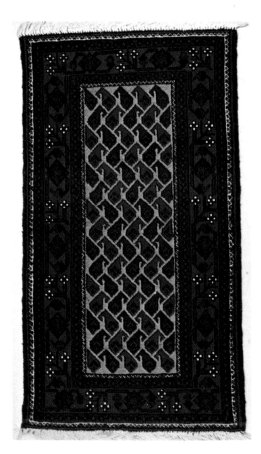

PLATE 64: *BALOUCH (Boteh Design)*
Woven in Iran, 3 ft. by 5 ft.
Courtesy of Mr. and Mrs. Richard LeNoir

94

PLATE 65: *BALOUCH (Prayer Design)*
Woven in Afghanistan, 3 ft. by 5 ft.
Courtesy of Mr. and Mrs. William Ennis

PLATE 66: *BALOUCH (Semi-Antique)*
Woven in Iran, 3 ft. by 5 ft.
Courtesy of Dr. Theodore Herbert

for their weaving of prayer rugs. Many different motifs may fill the *mihrab*, but the stylized Tree-of-life design is most commonly used. The running-dog or Greek key border is a common characteristic of most Balouchi rugs. (See Plates 64 and 66.)

As with Turkoman rugs and those made by the nomadic tribes of Iran, Balouchi rugs are woven on a horizontal loom. The warp thread may be either wool or cotton. The newer Balouchi rugs of Iran have a cotton warp and a thicker pile than those made in Afghanistan. The weft is usually single and made either of sheep's wool or a mixture of sheep's wool and goat's hair. The knot used is the Persian. The pile is of good-quality wool; camel's wool is used on rare occasions.

Semi-antique and antique Balouchi rugs often have at each end a wide *kelim*, which may be decorated with multicolored stripes or small motifs. Selvedges are double and made of black goat's hair. The colors of older rugs are more muted, with shades of dark red, brown, black, and camel; the newer rugs are somewhat brighter.

Both new and semi-antique Balouchi rugs are available. Most of these rugs are in small sizes (3 by 5 to 4 by 6 feet).

Caucasian Rugs

CAUCASIAN RUGS are a study all their own. Identifying a rug as Caucasian is not very difficult, since they have a woolen foundation, brilliant colors, and highly stylized, geometric motifs. Further classification as to town or region gets a little more complicated, as design and color are not always the clues to identification in Caucasian rugs as they are for the Persian rugs.

The Caucasus Mountains form a natural boundary between Europe and Asia, rising in the narrow strip of land between the Black and Caspian Seas. Writing in 1807, German anthropologist Johann Friederich Blumenbach stated that the inhabitants of the Caucasus Mountain region comprised the purest example of the "white" race, thereby deriving the term

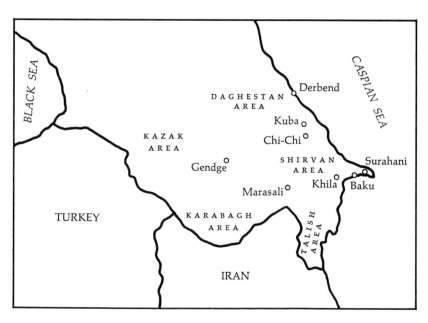

FIGURE 18:
*WEAVING
AREAS OF THE
CAUCASUS*

"Caucasian." It was also in the Caucasus Mountains that Zeus chained Prometheus for giving the fire of the gods to mortals.

Although the Caucasus has long been isolated from the rest of the world, there has been a great cultural interchange among the many ethnic groups and tribes inhabiting the area (see Figure 18). The southeast area (Karabagh, Baku, and part of Shirvan) reflects the Persian influence; in the northwest area (Kazak) there is a strong Armenian, Kurd, and Azeri Turk influence. In the northeast (Daghestan and Kuba) most inhabitants are Moslem. These nomadic and seminomadic tribesmen and villagers affect and are affected by the other tribes with whom they meet during the course of their travels. Although each village or tribe weaves designs unique to its area, there is a great exchange or borrowing of designs between the peoples. The diagonal stripe, which is used most often in Gendge, will appear in Kazak or even in Daghestan, for example.

Unlike the Persian and Turkoman rugs, dates have been quite often woven into Caucasian rugs. Dates based on the Christian calendar were woven into rugs from the western Caucasus regions by Armenian Christians. However, most dates are based on the Moslem calendar.

Caucasian rugs were imported in large quantities from the late 1800s until about 1935, when production for export ceased. After World War II, the Russians nationalized the weaving industry, and it was not until 1960 that a few Caucasian rugs (especially Kazak) started appearing on the western market.

Currently, rugs are made in many weaving centers throughout the Soviet Republics of Azerbaijan, Armenia, and Georgia. These rugs are quite expensive, owing to the high (45 percent) duty imposed by the United States government on all rugs from the Soviet Union.

KAZAK

KNOT:	*Turkish*
WARP:	*natural-colored wool, thick (three-ply)*
WEFT:	*wool usually dyed red, double*
PILE:	*long, thick heavy wool (shaggy appearance)*
FRINGE:	*looped at one end; knotted at the other*
SELVEDGE:	*several warp threads overcast with wool that has usually been dyed red*

The Kazaks are probably the most easily recognized of the Caucasian rugs because of their bold designs and brilliant colors. Woven in the western part of the Caucasus by Kurds and Armenians, their large-scaled designs may be dominated by a single or several medallions. The sizes are generally small, rarely more than 6 by 9 feet, and quite often almost square in shape. (See Plates 67 through 69.)

New Kazaks started appearing on the western market in the early 1960s. While more sophisticated in design, they lack the primitive charm and beauty of the older Kazaks.

PLATE 67: *KAZAK*
(Armenian)
3 ft. 11 in. by 8 ft. 7 in.

PLATE 68: *KAZAK (Prayer Design), 2 ft. by 3 ft. Courtesy of Mrs. Burch Thomas*

PLATE 69: *KAZAK, Kelim and Braided Fringe*

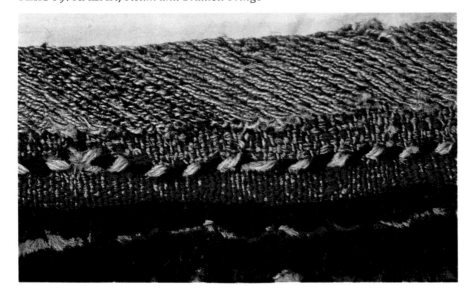

GENDGE *(Gendje, Geunge)*

KNOT:	*Turkish*
WARP:	*wool*
WEFT:	*wool; three, four, or more*
PILE:	*medium long*
FRINGE:	*looped at one end; knotted at the other*
SELVEDGE:	*several warp threads overcast with wool*

For centuries Gendge has been a trade center because of its strategic location on caravan routes and, more recently, on the rail line. It is situated halfway between the Black Sea and the Caspian Sea.

Structurally, the Gendge rugs differ very little from those of Kazak; however, quality may vary greatly, depending on the area in which the rugs were woven. Colors tend to be paler and designs smaller scaled than those of Kazak. The design most commonly associated with the Gendge is one of diagonal stripes covering the entire field. Each stripe contains a small repeating motif, such as a *boteh*. (See Plate 70.)

KARABAGH

KNOT: *Turkish*
WARP: *brown wool (occasionally cotton)*
WEFT: *wool (occasionally cotton)*
PILE: *medium long*
FRINGE: *looped at one end; knotted at the other*
SELVEDGE: *two warp threads usually overcast with wool*

Like those of Gendje, the rugs of Karabagh are similar in structure to the Kazak, to the extent that it is sometimes hard to tell the difference. The Karabaghs tend to be more floral, more finely knotted, and to have shorter pile than the Kazaks. The Karabagh area is located east and south of the Kazak area in the southern part of the Caucasus along the Iranian border.

The Chelaberd ("sunburst" or Eagle Kazak) contains one or more radial medallions in the field (see Plate 71). A strong Persian influence is evident in some of the designs; curvilinear (a Savonnerie-type floral) as well as rectilinear (Herati and *boteh*) motifs are used. (See Plate 72.) Although produced in the Karabagh area, these rugs possess features that are reminiscent of both Kazak and Karabagh. Opinions differ on the exact classification of these rugs as either Karabaghs or Kazaks. The general consensus is that they should be considered to be Karabaghs.

PLATE 71: *KARABAGH ("Chelaberd" or "Eagle Kazak"),*
5 ft. by 8 ft. Courtesy of Mr. and Mrs. Alan Johnson

The Chondoresk (Cloudband or Dragon Kazak) is subject to the same classification controversy as the Chelaberd. Many features are characteristic of both Kazaks and Karabaghs, but it also should be classified as a Karabagh. The design has a medallion or medallions that contain cloudbands or dragon-like figures, which, in turn, surround a small geometric motif.

PLATE 72: *KARABAGH (Portion), 5 ft. by 9 ft. Courtesy of Hower House*

TALISH

KNOT:	*Turkish*
WARP:	*natural-colored wool*
WEFT:	*natural-colored wool (occasionally dyed red or blue); double*
PILE:	*medium*
FRINGE:	*looped at one end; knotted at the other*
SELVEDGE:	*blue wool over several warp threads*

Talish is a mountainous area on the Caspian Sea, south of the Moghan Steppe. It is directly south of Shirvan and east of Karabagh.

Talish rugs are easily identified by their characteristic design and shape. The field is usually navy, although red or cream is also used. The field may be open, or it may be filled with rosettes and/or stars; the field may even have only a single rosette or star. The main border is also a distinguishing mark of the Talish, almost always white with large rosettes separated by small squares or stars (see Plate 73). The vast majority of rugs produced are runners, with sizes ranging up to approximately 12 feet in length.

PLATE 73: *TALISH, 3 ft. by 6 ft.*
Courtesy of Hower House

PLATE 74: *SHIRVAN*
4 ft. by 8 ft.

opposite, PLATE 75:
SHIRVAN
("Marasali" Prayer)
3 ft. by 4 ft.
Courtesy of
Mrs. Burch Thomas

SHIRVAN

KNOT:	*Turkish*
WARP:	*dark brown wool twisted with a single white strand*
WEFT:	*wool, white, or natural colored; occasionally cotton in newer rugs*
PILE:	*short*
FRINGE:	*looped at one end (often woven into a* kelim*); knotted at other*
SELVEDGE:	*several warp threads overcast with wool*

Vast numbers of rugs were woven in the Shirvan area in many different villages. As in the villages of Kuba, certain designs are woven that are unique to individual villages. Many different designs, such as large geometric medallions with eight-pointed stars or large, hooked octagons (see Plate 74), and many prayer rugs (see Plate 75) are found throughout the Shirvan area. One of the most unique designs is woven in the village of

Marasali: the field is filled with rows of pastel-colored *boteh*, each of which is encompassed by a serrated outline.

The Shirvan area is south of Kuba and southeast of the eastern slopes of the Greater Caucasus Mountain Range. The rugs of Shirvan are similar in color and design to those of Kuba, and are quite often mislabeled as Kabistans.

The most distinguishing feature of Shirvans is the warp thread. The three-ply warp is composed of two strands of dark brown wool that have entwined with a single strand of white wool. In addition, the warp threads lie horizontally to each other, as contrasted to the depressed warp threads of rugs from Kuba and Daghestan. This unique construction gives an almost flat appearance to the back of the rug.

The Shirvans are usually very finely knotted, with short pile. The colors tend to be more muted and subdued than in other Caucasian rugs.

BAKU

KNOT:	*Turkish*
WARP:	*brown wool*
WEFT:	*brown wool or a mixture of wool and cotton, double*
PILE:	*short*
FRINGE:	*knotted and cut at both ends*
SELVEDGE:	*blue wool or cotton over several warp threads*

Baku is the capital of the Soviet Republic of Azerbaijan. With a population of over one million people, Baku is the Soviet Union's fifth largest city. Located on the Aspheron Peninsula in the Caspian Sea, it is the center of the area's great oil industry.

The *boteh* is the design most often associated with the rugs of Baku. These *boteh* are of many different colors and the medallion (when used) is a pale blue. The colors used in Baku are more muted than those of other areas in the Caucasus. The rugs of the Baku area are noted for the many shades of blue used, from a light blue to a beautiful shade of turquoise. The ground is often a dark blue or black. The sizes tend to be small, and are rarely more than 6 feet by 9 feet.

Khila and Surahani have been the two most important Baku-area villages. The rugs of Khila contain a design with *boteh*, and the rugs of Surahani have a design that contains stars and rosettes. In Surahani, weaving is currently done in nationalized carpet factories. Traditional designs form the basis for the weaving. The sizes produced are typically 6 by 9 feet and smaller.

KUBA

KNOT:	*Turkish*
WARP:	*natural-colored wool or cotton*
WEFT:	*natural-colored wool or cotton*
PILE:	*short*
FRINGE:	*several rows of knots with cut fringe*
SELVEDGE:	*several warp threads overcast with blue or white wool*

The town of Kuba lies near the Caspian Sea, halfway between Derbend and Baku. Rugs are made in a number of villages in the Kuba area, each of which tends to weave its own design. (For example: Sejshour weaves a design with large diagonal cross beams in the field of the rug; Perepedil weaves a design which resembles a ram's head.) As a result, there is no single design that distinguishes a Kuba from other Caucasian rugs.

An important differentiating feature is the narrow *kelims* at both ends
of the rug that are reinforced with a blue Soumak stitch. The Kuba rugs are
generally finely woven, and possess a thick foundation because of alternating warp threads that are depressed into the body of the rug. (See
Plate 76.)

Chi-Chi was the most prolific of the Kuba-area villages. The size of
its field tends to be restricted because of the numerous borders used. Small
stepped, hooked polygons situated in rows adorn the field of the rug.

PLATE 76: *KUBA*
4 ft. by 6 ft.
Courtesy of
Mrs. William
Campbell, Sr.

DAGHESTAN

KNOT: *Turkish*
WARP: *natural-colored wool or cotton*
WEFT: *natural-colored wool or cotton*
PILE: *medium to medium long*
FRINGE: *three or four rows of knots with cut fringe at both ends*
SELVEDGE: *warp overcast with blue wool*

The Daghestan area, now the Soviet state of Daghestan, occupies the northeast slopes of the Greater Caucasus Mountains. It is the northernmost of the Caucasian rug-producing areas.

Enormous numbers of prayer rugs were woven with a cream-colored field filled with small geometrical flowers contained in a trellis. Another design quite common to Daghestan is that of diagonal bands containing small hooked motifs and covering the entire field of the rug. Many of these rugs have been confused with Shirvans and Kabistans, and a careful study of the structure should be made before classification of a rug. Rugs currently made in the Daghestan area contain bold, geometric medallions and employ small motifs scattered throughout the field (see Plate 77).

The body of Daghestan rugs is quite thick because of the depression of alternating warp threads into the body of the rug. The warp threads have a distinctive knotting characteristic of three or four rows of knots, giving a honeycomb effect, before the cut fringe at the ends.

PLATE 77:
DAGHESTAN
2 ft. by 4 ft.
Courtesy of Dr. and
Mrs. John Campbell

DERBEND

KNOT:	*Turkish*
WARP:	*wool, cotton, or a mixture of both*
WEFT:	*wool, two or three strands*
PILE:	*heavy wool, medium long*
FRINGE:	*knotted at both ends*
SELVEDGE:	*two warp threads overcast with blue wool*

Located on the coast of the Caspian Sea, the town of Derbend is surrounded by the Daghestan area. In general, the rugs of Derbend were inferior to those of the whole of Daghestan. They were loosely woven with dark colors, navy blue and madder red. Repeated small geometric motifs or three geometric medallions were often used in Derbend designs; however, a variety of designs were used.

Turkoman Rugs

THE VAST AREA referred to as Turkestan receives its name from the people of the Turkish stock, called Turkomans, who have inhabited the region since 500 A.D. For centuries, trade routes through Turkestan have linked the Far East with Europe. The riches of China were brought to Europe by Marco Polo as early as 1295 A.D. Turkestan has had little direct influence on Europe and the western world, although its land has had a long history of conquest. In the fourth century B.C., Alexander the Great was the first in a series of famous conquerors who subjugated Turkestan. Genghis Khan ruled its large expanses in the thirteenth century, and Tamerlane established the capital of his great Mongol Empire at Samarkand in the fourteenth century. Russia's gradual conquest of Turkestan began in the seventeenth century; by the middle of the nineteenth century most of western Turkestan was under Russian rule. For the most part of the nineteenth century eastern Turkestan was under Chinese rule.

In the past, Turkoman rugs were woven in the vast area of central Asia that extends from the Gobi Desert in China on the east, to the Caspian Sea on the west. The Kazak Steppe in the Soviet Republic of Kazak bounds the area on the north; Iran's Kopet Dagh Mountains and Afghanistan's Hindu Kush and Paropamisus Mountains are the southern limits (see Figure 19).

The many tribes of this region have traditionally been nomadic and virtually unaffected by political boundaries. This way of life changed in the early 1930s, when the Russians established, and began to strictly enforce, the Soviet borders. After the vast majority of Turkestan land fell under Soviet control, the nomadic Turkoman could no longer freely migrate and thus was forced to change his traditional life-style.

Today, most of the Turkoman weaving is centered in Afghanistan. A few tribes of Tekke and Yomud in the Persian Steppe of northeast Iran also make the traditional Turkoman rugs. Some weaving is done by Turkoman tribes in the Soviet Union, but the high (45 percent) duty imposed is generally effective in restricting import of these rugs to the U.S. market. Current Turkoman rugs are labeled with their country of origin (as are all recent Oriental rugs); one result of this practice has been to de-emphasize the specific tribal classification of the rugs, and to emphasize their identification under the broader term "Turkoman."

Turkoman rugs are unmistakable in design; geometric motifs, *guls* unique to each tribe, are repeated in rows throughout the field of the rug. Figure 20 shows the most commonly encountered major *guls* (motifs).

The major variation to the repeated-*gul* design of Turkoman rugs is that of the *hatchlou* (or *katchli*), most often woven by members of the Yomud, Tekke, and Ersari (Afghan) tribes. In the *hatchlou* design, the field is divided into quadrants by two perpendicular strips or bars, resulting in a cross-like form (see Plate 78).

The quadrants are filled either with motifs resembling candlesticks or candelabras (Tekke or Ersari), or with small lozenge shapes (Yomud). The motifs contained in the bars and borders of the *hatchlou* design are characteristic of those associated with the rug's tribal origins. Rug dealers

FIGURE 19: *TURKOMAN TRIBAL LOCATIONS*

tend to label all Turkoman-*gul* rugs regardless of age as Bukharas* whether they are from Pakistan, Afghanistan, Iran, or the Soviet Union. Repeated-*gul* designs are termed "Royal Bukharas"; *hatchlou* designs are called "Princess Bukharas." Few if any rugs were woven in Bukhara; the town was simply a marketplace for the rugs of several of the Turkoman tribes.

Like the nomadic women of Iran, Turkoman women weave their rugs on horizontal or ground looms. The warp and weft threads are of wool or goat's hair, or a mixture of both, and the pile is generally a good-quality wool or camel's hair. With few exceptions, Turkoman rugs are woven with the Persian knot; the Yomud tribe, however, characteristically used the

* Alternate spellings are Bukara and Bokhara.

PLATE 78: *HATCHLOU DESIGN–TEKKE (with Prayer Arch)*

FIGURE 20: *MAJOR TURKOMAN GULS*

Turkish knot. Red is the dominant color, with specific shade varying from tribe to tribe.

Turkoman weavers were not averse to the use of aniline dyes, and some semi-antique Turkomans exhibit the characteristic signs of fading associated with these dyes. Proper caution should be used (see Dyes, pp. 24-25).

Antique Turkoman rugs are rare. Semi-antique Turkomans are not widely available, but may be encountered. Because of their increased popularity, new rugs from Afghanistan are coming to the U.S. market in quantities larger than ever before.

SALOR

KNOT: *Persian*
WARP: *light-colored wool or goat's hair*
WEFT: *light-colored wool, single or double*
PILE: *short, tightly knotted, fine-quality wool*
FRINGE: *narrow* kelim *with plain fringe*
SELVEDGE: *double overcast with wool*

The Salor tribe was once the wealthiest and most prestigious of the Turkoman tribes. They occupied the oasis land surrounding Merv from the late seventeenth century until driven from their homelands by the Tekke tribe in 1856. By 1870, tribal wars and disputes had dispersed the Salor population, and many Salors were absorbed into Sariq and Tekke tribes. A small group of Salors still reside around Marutshak in northern Afghanistan.*

The Salor *gul* is octagonal with spiked projections pointing both inward and outward from its rim. A smaller octagon appears at the center of the *gul.* The secondary *guls* used in Salor rugs resemble the major *guls* of the Tekke and Sariq tribes. The colors used vary from a rose wine to a mahogany. The Salor tribe used the finest-quality wool, and their weaving technique was the best of all the Turkoman tribes. (See Plate 79.)

A Salor-like *gul* is woven in Afghanistan today by Sariq tribes. The rugs in which these *guls* appear resemble the traditional Sariq rugs in colors and skirt ornamentation, and are marketed as Sariq Mauri.

---

* Eiland, Murray, *Oriental Rugs: A Comprehensive Guide* (Greenwich, Conn.: New York Graphic Society, Ltd., 1976), p. 144.

PLATE 79: *SALOR Chuval (Bag Face) 2 ft. by 4 ft. Courtesy of Dr. and Mrs. John Campbell*

SARIQ *(Saryk, Sarik)*

KNOT:	*Persian or Turkish*
WARP:	*wool with alternating warp threads slightly depressed*
WEFT:	*wool, double*
PILE:	*wool, medium short*
FRINGE:	*wide* kelim *with plain fringe at both ends*
SELVEDGE:	*double selvedge overcast with dark blue wool*

Since the late nineteenth century, a group of Sariq tribes have lived along the Murghab River south of Merv (in the Pinde district), around Marutshak; another group resides between Maimana and Qaisar. With the gradual dispersal of the Salor tribes after the fall of Merv in 1856, many Salors made new homes among the Sariq tribes. These Salors continued to weave their *guls* while probably adopting some of the Sariq weaving characteristics, which adds to the confusion of trying to pinpoint an exact tribal identification. Currently in Afghanistan, Sariq tribes weave a rug with a Salor *gul* and Sariq structural characteristics. See Sariq Mauri, p. 123.

The Sariq *gul* has an octagon shape similar to that of the Tekke. The *gul* is generally divided into quadrants with the center of the *gul* containing a cross-like motif. The secondary *guls* resemble those used by the Tekke. Sariq rugs were deep purplish brown, colors darker than those used in most Turkoman rugs. (See Plate 80.)

YOMUD *(Yomut)*

KNOT: *Turkish, occasionally Persian*
WARP: *wool or goat's hair, white or light colored*
WEFT: *wool, double (single in new Iranian Yomuds)*
PILE: *wool*
FRINGE: *wide* kelim *with either braided or plain fringe*
SELVEDGE: *double overcast with wool*

At the beginning of the nineteenth century, the Yomud tribes resided along the eastern shores of the Caspian Sea. Since then, the many Yomud tribes have separated and become widely scattered over northeast Iran, Afghanistan, and Russia. Even though this dispersal has caused a greater variation in the Yomud designs than those of other Turkoman tribes, most of the Yomud *guls* retain their characteristic latch hook. This distinctive ornamentation reflects the Yomud's original proximity to the Caucasus region, where the use of the latch hook is so prevalent. Since World War II, the Yomud tribes living in Iran have woven not only the traditional Yomud *gul* but also a Tekke-type *gul*.

The Yomud *gul* is a diamond-shaped motif with latched or serrated edges (see Plate 81). The *gul* may be divided into quarters; the size of the

PLATE 81: *YOMUD*
6 ft. 3 in. by 4 ft. 4 in.

opposite, PLATE 82
YOMUD
(Hatchlou Design)
4 ft. by 5 ft.
Courtesy of Mrs.
Burch Thomas

116

gul varies from tribe to tribe. In addition to the traditional Turkoman *gul* designs, a *hatchlou* design rug, with or without an arch, is also woven by Yomuds (see Plate 82). At the ends of Yomud rugs, between the borders and the *kelim,* are wide bands or skirts woven with a slightly different design from that which is used in the side borders. These skirts are decorated with a wide variety of designs.

The reds used by Yomud tribes vary from reddish brown to a wine red. White is generally used in the primary border and appears more often in Yomuds than in other Turkoman rugs.

Sizes vary greatly according to use; many saddlebags and tent bags as well as room-size rugs are available. The antique and semi-antique pieces are rare, but recent examples of Yomud weaving are available on the market.

TEKKE

KNOT: *Persian*
WARP: *wool*
WEFT: *wool or goat's hair, double*
PILE: *short, fine-quality wool*
FRINGE: *narrow* kelim, *usually red with small motifs*
SELVEDGE: *double overcast with wool usually dyed navy blue*

In the last half of the nineteenth century, Tekke tribes occupied the Akhal and the Merv Oases (now located in the Soviet Republic of Turkoman), as well as most of the land in between. The Russians defeated the Tekke tribes at Merv in 1884, and many Tekke tribes migrated south into Afghanistan. Border controls were tightened in 1930, making further migration impossible.

The distinguishing characteristic of the Tekke rug is its *gul*, an octagonal motif divided symmetrically into quadrants. Each *gul* contains an eight-pointed design (although a six-pointed design is often used in newer rugs) emitting spiked projections. Each *gul* is usually connected to neighboring *guls* by horizontal and vertical lines, which run through the field of the carpet. Spider-like minor, or secondary, *guls* occupy the spaces between the rows and columns of the major Tekke *guls*. (See Figure 21.)

Today, weaving of the traditional Tekke *gul* is no longer limited to members of the Tekke tribe; it has recently been woven in Iran by several Yomud tribes (the rugs of which are called Bukharas or, more generally, Turkomans), in Afghanistan by Sariq and Ersari tribes (whose Tekke-*gul* rugs are referred to as Mauri; see pp. 123-124), and in Pakistan (whose Turkoman-*gul* rugs are also termed Bukharas). The Tekke *gul* is the one used most often in those Bukhara rugs that are woven in Pakistan.

The Tekke rugs of Iran are usually woven with a cotton warp and weft. The Tekke rugs made in Afghanistan have a fine white or light-colored wool used for both the warp and weft threads. The pile of the Tekke rugs made in both Iran and Afghanistan is excellent-quality, hard-wearing wool.

FIGURE 21: *MINOR TURKOMAN GULS*

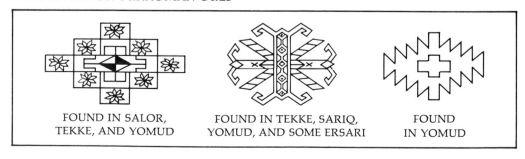

| FOUND IN SALOR, TEKKE, AND YOMUD | FOUND IN TEKKE, SARIQ, YOMUD, AND SOME ERSARI | FOUND IN YOMUD |

Three borders generally surround the field of the rug; the center, wider border contains a series of octagonal shapes. Outside the borders, at the top and at the bottom of a Tekke rug, will be a wide panel or skirt, usually containing a hooked diamond motif. Ground colors are either a brick red or a dark wine. White, burnt orange, and dark blue are the most common motif colors. (See Plate 83.)

The Tekke is the most prevalent of the antique and semi-antique Turkoman rugs. They can be found with either the Tekke *gul* or the *hatchlou* ("cross") design in 3 by 5 to 4 by 6 feet sizes as well as saddlebags and bag faces. New Tekke rugs come in a wide variety of sizes.

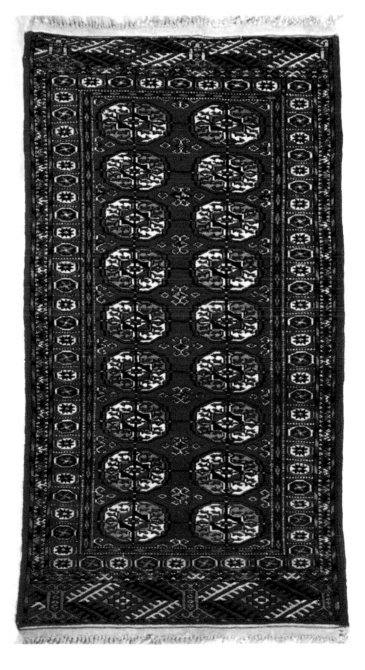

PLATE 83: *TEKKE 2 ft. by 4 ft. Courtesy of Mr. and Mrs. William Ennis*

ERSARI

KNOT: *Persian (several rows of Turkish knots are often found along the two sides)*

WARP: *gray-colored wool or goat's hair*

WEFT: *dark-colored wool of goat's hair, double*

PILE: *thick, excellent-quality wool*

FRINGE: *wide* kelim *usually red, with knotted fringe at both ends*

SELVEDGE: *double selvedge overcast with dark-colored wool or goat's hair*

For several hundred years Ersari tribes have lived along the banks of the Amu Darya, a river which forms a portion of the boundary between Afghanistan and the Soviet Union. Ersari tribes could be found as far north as Chardzhou (160 miles inside the Soviet Union) and scattered throughout northeast Afghanistan. Although clans of Ersari have resided in Afghanistan since the late seventeenth century, mass migrations of Ersari occurred from 1874, when Khiva fell to the Russians, to the closing of the Russo-Afghan border in the early 1930s.

As a result, the Ersaris constitute the largest Turkoman population in Afghanistan today. Important to the Afghanistan economy, Ersaris are the principal rug-weaving tribes, as well as a significant factor in sheepherding. Sheepskin and carpets are Afghanistan's major exports.

Ersari rugs usually possess a typical Turkoman-style *gul* design. The most common of the many Ersari *guls* is a quartered octagon encompassing a polygon; each quadrant contains at least one dog-shaped motif. Yet Ersaris weave a wide variety of designs, ranging from the geometric and bold *filpoi* ("elephant's foot") *gul* of the "Afghan," to the floral and the Herati pattern of the Beshire.

The Persian is the primary knot used by the Ersari tribes. A unique feature of Ersari rugs is the Turkish knots that are the last several knots on each side. Every other warp thread is slightly depressed. The selvedges are often double and overcast with goat's hair, in fashion similar to those of the Balouchi tribes. Ersari rugs are brighter in color than most other Turkoman rugs; yellow and blue predominate as secondary colors. (See Plate 84.)

The sizes of Ersari rugs vary from small mat and bag faces to room size. The antique Ersari are rather rare. Although not common, the semi-antique Ersari rugs are more easily obtained. For the new production of the Ersari, see the section, *Recent Turkoman Rugs of Afghanistan*, pp. 123-124.

PLATE 84: *ERSARI, 2 ft. by 4 ft.*
Courtesy of Mr. and Mrs. Clair Harrah

AFGHAN

Afghan rugs were made by Ersari tribes regardless of location of the weavers (either Afghanistan or Russia). "Afghan" refers to design (the *gul* motif), rather than country of origin.

Afghan rugs have either a single column or several columns of repeated *filpoi* ("elephant's foot") *guls.* The *filpoi* is a large octagonal *gul*, which may range in diameter from 10 to 15 inches. Each *gul* is quartered, with each segment containing a trefoil or treelike design. The trefoils extend from a

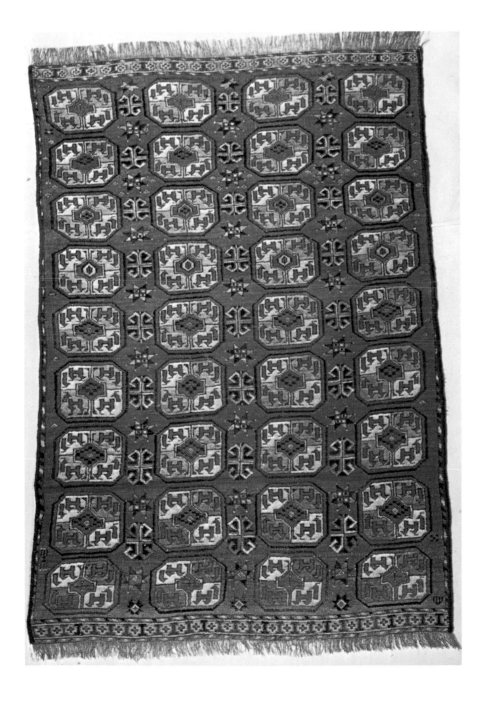

central polygon or square. The same *filpoi* design used in the Afghan is also used in a rug called the Khiva. The only difference between the Afghan and the Khiva is in quality; the Khiva is more finely woven.

Wool warp and weft threads are used. Often the wool is from goats rather than sheep. The pile is a good-quality heavy wool that has been knotted with the Persian knot.

The ground of most Afghans is a deep red with designs outlined in black, dark blue, or brown (see Plate 85). In recent years, a "golden Afghan" has appeared on the market. Some of these rugs were originally red, but were heavily bleached to obtain a yellow hue. A careful inspection of the base of the pile will reveal remnants of the original red color. The bleached wool has been weakened and the wearing qualities impaired, so caution should be exercised in buying. True "golden Afghans" are woven with yellow yarn and possess the same excellent wearing qualities of the red Afghans.

Afghans are solid, durable rugs that are relatively inexpensive. They are available in virtually all sizes.

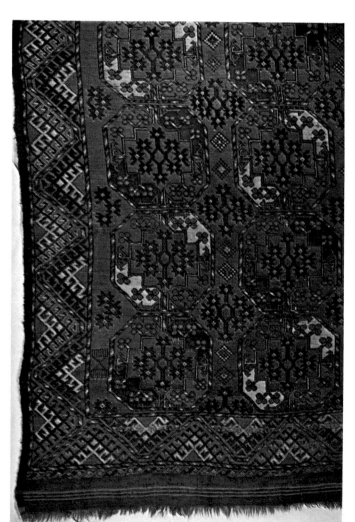

PLATE 85: *AFGHAN
(Portion)
6 ft. by 9 ft.
Courtesy of Mr. and
Mrs. Ted Trikilis*

RECENT TURKOMAN RUGS
OF AFGHANISTAN

MAURI

KNOT:	*Persian*
WARP:	*wool (white or light gray)*
WEFT:	*dark wool*
PILE:	*short, evenly clipped*
FRINGE:	*wide kelim (may be red) with knotted fringe at both ends*
SELVEDGE:	*overcast with dark blue or black wool*

Rugs made in Afghanistan since World War II are classified in a way different from the semi-antique and antique Turkoman rugs. They are indeed Turkoman rugs, but further classification is necessary for several reasons. First, during the border disputes, there were many migrations and resettlings of the Turkoman tribes and their subtribes. Remnants of one tribe often merged with those of another, finally settling outside each of their traditional homelands. Although these Turkomans continued weaving rugs, they often adopted and adapted the antique *guls*. For example, a Tekke *design* rug not woven by a Tekke tribe is labeled *Mauri* rather than Tekke. Second, new designs have emerged, owing to their increased popularity as well as the commercial motive of weaving designs to meet consumer tastes.

There are two principal types of Turkoman rugs woven in Afghanistan today. The Mauri is an excellent-quality carpet, usually with a Tekke *gul* design. (See Plate 86.) The Daulatabad, also of fine quality, rug is woven with the *filpoi* design.

Mauri rugs are woven in many areas throughout northern Afghanistan. Tekke-design Mauri rugs are woven in Marutshak, Mazar-i-Sharif, and Herat and its surrounding province. Several carpets with other *guls* are also given the Mauri label. For example, the Sariq Mauri, woven primarily by the Sariq tribe, has a Salor-like *gul*, Sariq colors, and skirt designs reminiscent of antique Sariq rugs.

Like the Mauri rugs, the Daulatabads are made in various weaving centers throughout northern Afghanistan. They too may be typed according to the various adaptations in the *gul* design. (See Plate 87.)

The majority of all Turkoman rugs now being woven are made in Afghanistan. The focus of our discussion of Afghanistan Turkomans has been the Mauri and Daulatabad, since these excellent-quality rugs comprise the majority of the rug production for the U.S. market. Mauri and Daulatabad are not representative of all Afghanistani weaving; medium- and lower-

quality rugs are being produced in Aktsha and Shibergan. Much of the weaving comes from numerous small subtribes and families; these rugs have not been discussed because of their great variation and individually insignificant production.

Excellent-quality Turkoman rugs are being woven across the Afghan border in the Russian provinces of Turkoman and Uzbek; few are found on the U.S. market because of the extremely high (45 percent) duty imposed. The current rug production of the Yomud and Tekke tribes of northeast Iran has been discussed previously in the respective sections.

EASTERN TURKESTAN

KNOT: *Persian*

WARP: *gray wool (may vary from light to dark)*

WEFT: *dark brown or black wool*

PILE: *heavy coarse wool; medium to medium long*

FRINGE: *wide kelim (usually red) with knotted fringe at both ends*

SELVEDGE: *double selvedge overcast with dark wool*

The Tien Shan Mountains separate Eastern and Western Turkestan. Eastern Turkestan, often called Chinese Turkestan, is located in what is now the Sinkiang Province of the People's Republic of China. Most of the inhabitants are of Turkish descent; Chinese make up only 10 percent of the population.

Rugs from this region have often been referred to as Samarkands. Included among rugs of this region are those of Khotan, Kashgar, and Yarkand. Like Bukhara, Samarkand was located on ancient caravan routes and

PLATE 87: *DAULATABAD (Prayer Design)*
3 ft. by 5 ft.

for centuries has been a marketplace for rugs. Samarkands reflect a definite Chinese influence; rounded medallions, Chinese geometrical patterns, and other Chinese motifs are common to rugs of this area. (See Plate 88.)

Very few Eastern Turkestan rugs have ever been imported for the U.S. market. They do, however, appear on the London market.

The colors used are peach, light blues and grays, steel blue, browns, and golds. The wools are soft and the weave rather coarse; the sizes tend to be small (6 by 9 feet, and smaller).

KNOT:	*Persian, Turkish (in older rugs)*
WARP:	*cotton*
WEFT:	*cotton, two or more*
PILE:	*soft, silky wool*
FRINGE:	kelim *with looped fringe at one end and* kelim *with plain fringe at the other*
SELVEDGE:	*double overcast with wool*

PLATE 88: *KHOTAN, 3 ft. by 5 ft. Courtesy of Mr. and Mrs. William Ennis*

126

Rugs from

China, Pakistan, and India

CHINA

KNOT:	*Persian*
WARP:	*cotton*
WEFT:	*cotton, double*
PILE:	*wool, medium short to medium long in length*
FRINGE:	*kelim with knotted fringe at both ends*
SELVEDGE:	*overcast with wool*

UNTIL 1973, trade between the U.S. and the People's Republic of China was illegal. The only Chinese rugs available were either used, from estates; or new, made in Hong Kong or Taiwan (Nationalist China). Of the Chinese carpets available on the U.S. market, the majority have come from two major weaving centers: Peiking and Tientsin. Rugs from Tientsin have been more numerous in production and in export.

The Peiking rugs made before World War II generally had a blue or white ground; several shades of blue, white, and yellow were used in the motifs and borders. *Shou*-sign center medallions were often used, with various other symbols found throughout the rest of the field (see Plate 89).

The Tientsin rugs made before World War II had a thicker pile and a slightly tighter weave than those made in Peiking. A wider range of colors were also used, including almost any color imaginable. Many different Chinese designs and symbols were used in the rugs from Tientsin: dragons, vase of flowers, temples, and so forth. Sometimes the design, such as the bough of a tree, will seem to extend off the carpet. Some Tientsin rugs were woven with no border. (See Plate 90.)

Since trade was established with the People's Republic of China in 1973, new Chinese carpets have been appearing on the New York market. The

PLATE 90: *TIENTSIN*
2 ft. 11 in. by 5 ft. 8 in.
Courtesy of Mr. and
Mrs. Donald Dieterich

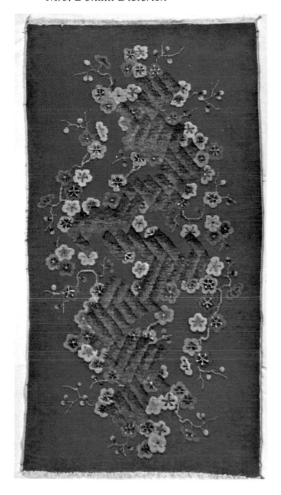

PLATE 91: *PEIKING*
2 ft. 3 in. by 4 ft. 6 in.

price of these rugs is relatively high, due in part to the 45-percent import
duty levied. These new Chinese rugs have standardized designs, the traditional Chinese motifs as well as a French Aubusson design. The motifs
are often accented by the pile's being "sculptured" or "carved" (see Plate
91). A multitude of color combinations and sizes are woven.

PAKISTAN

KNOT: *Persian*
WARP: *cotton (wool in older rugs)*
WEFT: *cotton (wool in older rugs)*
PILE: *silky wool, short to medium short in length*
·FRINGE: kelim *with knotted fringe at both ends*
SELVEDGE: *overcast with wool*

Oriental rugs from Pakistan are becoming increasingly popular on the U.S. market because of their reasonable price, crisp designs, and silky appearance. Many U.S. customers are finding them attractive alternatives to the higher-priced Persian rugs.

All designs used in Pakistani rugs are adopted from those of other weaving centers. Designs that employ the Turkoman *guls*, especially the

PLATE 92: *PAKISTANI PRAYER (Ghiordes Prayer Design) 2 ft. 5 in. by 4 ft. 1 in. Courtesy of Mr. Russell Herbert*

130

PLATE 93: *PAKISTAN BUKHARA*
3 ft. 1 in. by 5 ft. 2 in.

Tekke, are the most popular. These rugs are referred to as Bukharas; they are classified as "Royal" Bukharas (repeated *guls*) and "Princess" Bukharas (*hatchlou* design), terms which are unrelated to quality. Other designs are also woven and beautifully executed in Pakistani rugs; these include the Ghiordes Prayer and the Saff from Turkey, Kazak and other Caucasian designs, and Kashan-inspired designs (both the medallion and the prayer) from Iran. (See Plates 92 and 93.) As with all Oriental rugs, these must be labeled with their country of origin.

The carpets from Pakistan are finely knotted and the woolen pile has a lustrous appearance resulting from a light chemical wash. This wool is not as durable as that used in most Persian rugs. However, the quality of Pakistani rugs does vary greatly, and the best Pakistani rugs are superior to the lower quality Persian rugs.

The attractively low cost of an Oriental rug from Pakistan (as compared to a Persian rug, for example) may be attributed to cheap labor and government subsidies. As a result, an Oriental rug from Pakistan can provide substantial value at a reasonable price.

INDIA

KNOT:	*Persian*
WARP:	*cotton (jute in some older rugs)*
WEFT:	*cotton, double*
PILE:	*wool, medium in length*
FRINGE:	*knotted at both ends*
SELVEDGE:	*overcast with wool*

Carpet-weaving in India was started in the sixteenth century. The Mongol emperors brought Persian weavers to their royal courts to establish rug-weaving. These early Indian rugs were woven with the beautiful patterns of Kashan and Isfahan.

New carpets made in India, like those made in Pakistan, employ a variety of designs copied from other weaving centers. Chinese and antique Savonnerie and Aubusson patterns are common, as well as the Persian designs of Herez, Tabriz, and Kashan. (See Plates 94 and 95.) These carpets are identified by the prefix *Indo*, such as Indo-Savonnerie and Indo-Tabriz.

The weaving industry in India is highly commercialized. Many U.S. wholesalers contract with Indian weaving firms for large quantities of standardized-design rugs.

The quality of Indian rugs has improved; however, there is a wide range of quality available. Rugs woven in India are generally not as finely knotted and designs not as well executed as those made in Pakistan or in most parts of Iran. The wool is not as durable as that used in most Pakistani or Persian rugs, and is rather lusterless by comparison.

PLATE 95:
*INDO–CHINESE
DESIGN
3 ft. 1 in. by 5 ft. 1 in.
Courtesy of Dr. and
Mrs. Wilbur Veith*

Kelims and Pileless Carpets

KELIMS ARE WOVEN (as opposed to knotted) carpets and, hence, are pile-less. They are the oldest form of handmade rugs; in the past they have been neither widely available nor very popular. Yet recently they have gained acceptance and increased demand in the United States.

Woven carpets are not unique to a specific location; they are found throughout Iran, Turkestan, the Caucasus, Turkey, and elsewhere. These pileless carpets were made to be used as inexpensive floor coverings or as blankets or saddlebags.

The design of a Kelim is formed by colored weft threads, which are woven back and forth through the warp threads. In a design, when wefts of two different colors meet, small slits will occur, because the thread of a particular color is woven back to complete its own colored area of the design (see Figure 22).

Woven by Kurdistan tribes, Senna Kelims, considered the finest made, are made with a Herati design almost identical to the Senna rug (see Plate 96). The Balouchi tribes of Khurasan weave a Kelim with a design that has been brocaded or embroidered. This is done by the addition of an

FIGURE 22

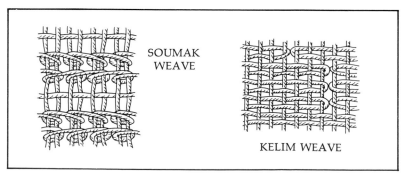

SOUMAK WEAVE

KELIM WEAVE

opposite,
PLATE 96:
SENNA KELIM
4 ft. by 6 ft.
Courtesy of
Dr. and Mrs.
L.A. Graham

134

PLATE 97: *BALOUCHI KELIM*
2 ft. by 3 ft.

opposite, PLATE 98:
SHIRVAN PALAS
3 ft. by 5 ft.
Courtesy of Hower Ho

extra weft thread, which is used for the embroidering of a design on the ground of the rug. (See Plate 97.)

In the Caucasus, Kelims are referred to as *palas*. These rugs are generally woven in the Skirvan area; however, they are also found throughout the Caucasus. The *palas* are woven in the same manner as the Persian and Anatolian *kelims*. (See Plate 98.)

Soumaks are another type of pileless rug woven in the Caucasus and in parts of Iran. They possess two types of weft threads. The colored design, or weft, thread is passed over (for example) four warp threads and brought back under two (similar to a chain stitch). Each row of colored wefts alternate in a different direction, giving a herringbone effect. The other weft thread is used to strengthen the carpet and support the design weft threads. When the color thread is changed, the thread is pulled through to the back of the carpet and left to hang, thus leaving only one side of the Soumak usable. (See Plates 99 and 100.)

The Sileh is woven in the southern Caucasus (Shirvan or Karabagh), using the Soumak technique. The designs consist of rows of large angular S motifs, which are filled with the same S designs, only smaller. A Sileh generally consists of two identical pieces that have been sewn together.

136

PLATE 99:
SOUMAK CAMEL BAG
3 ft. by 4 ft.

PLATE 100:
ARDEBIL SOUMAK
4 ft. by 6 ft.
Courtesy of Dr. and
Mrs. Wilbur Veith

9 *Buying and Caring for an Oriental Rug*

An Oriental rug should be purchased and cared for as a work of art. There are no hard-and-fast rules that govern the buying of an Oriental rug; each rug is unique. An Oriental rug properly cared for is a lifetime investment, a hedge against inflation, and a beautiful yet utilitarian work of art.

Buying an Oriental Rug

When purchasing an Oriental rug, the buyer should consider many factors. A reputable dealer can be very helpful, but the final appraisal and decision must be made by the purchaser.

BEFORE BUYING

In order to make the best possible decision when buying an Oriental rug, the purchaser should keep in mind several questions:

What is the purpose of buying an Oriental rug? Is it strictly utilitarian, a decorative accent, or an art investment? If the purpose of the rug is strictly utilitarian, will the rug be in a heavy traffic pattern?

What is the price range? The buyer should keep in mind the upper limit that he is willing to spend; this may narrow the available choices.

Can the rug be examined thoroughly? Often at auctions or house sales, hasty decisions are forced before a careful inspection of a rug can be made.

Can the rug be returned? A rug should be taken home to see if it creates the desired effect. If not, can the rug be exchanged or returned for a full refund? Most reputable Oriental rug dealers allow a free home trial for up to two weeks, with no obligation.

Does the seller guarantee the rug? There are traveling rug auctions that may only be in town for several days. The buyer has no recourse if the rug purchased is misrepresented or has serious or objectionable flaws. At house sales, for example, the rug is sold "as is," and the seller assumes no responsibility.

In short, the buyer should not be in such a hurry to buy that careful deliberation cannot be given. Also, a name normally associated with quality (such as Tabriz) does not guarantee that a specific rug of that type will be a quality rug. Quality varies even within weaving centers.

Machine-Made Oriental-Design Rugs

Rugs of Oriental *design* are widely available. Oriental-design rugs are not Oriental rugs; hand-*knotting* is the primary requirement of the Oriental rug. Knot loops may easily be seen by spreading the pile (see Plates 101 and 102). Oriental-design rugs are made by machine, and their pile attached by being glued or stitched. The designs and motifs of these rugs have been adapted from the traditional designs of Persian, Turkoman, and Chinese carpets.

Identifying the Oriental-design rug can be easily done in several ways.

PLATE 101: *The pile has been spread to show that each strand of wool has been tied to a pair of warp threads. (Alternating warp threads are depressed.) Tabriz carpet with Ghiordes knot.*

PLATE 102: *The pile of this machine-made carpet has been spread to show that the pile is attached without knots.*

PLATE 103: *The back of a hand-knotted (Tabriz) rug.*

PLATE 104: *The back of a machine-made Oriental design rug.*

When seen from the back, the design of a machine-made rug is vague or indistinct; it may have a backing (such as jute) covering the back of the rug. The design of a hand-knotted rug is clear on both front and back (see Plates 103 and 104).

Because of the hand-knotting process, there is a slight variation in each knot. The effects of these variations can be seen in the irregularities in the rows of knots, when observed from the back. The back of the machine-made rug displays a machine-like precision and an unvarying uniform appearance.

The fringe and selvedge offer other points for comparison. The fringe of the true Oriental consists of the loose ends of the rug's warp threads (some old Oriental rugs may have been refringed; see "fringe," p. 144); the fringe may be either knotted or plain. By contrast, the fringe of the machine-made rug has been overcast or sewn onto the carpet. (See Plates 105 and 106.) The sides of the machine-made rugs are bound (machine-stitched), unlike the cotton or wool hand overcasting on the genuine Oriental. (See Plates 107 and 108.)

PLATE 105: *The knotted fringe of a Tabriz rug.*

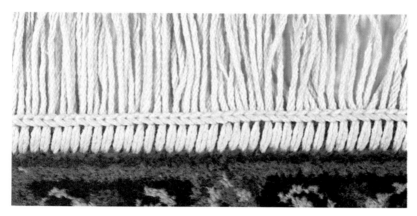

PLATE 106: *The overcast fringe of a machine-made Oriental-design rug. Fringe of this type will never be seen on a hand-knotted rug.*

PLATE 107: *The selvedge (hand overcast) on the side of a hand-knotted (Joshaghan) rug.*

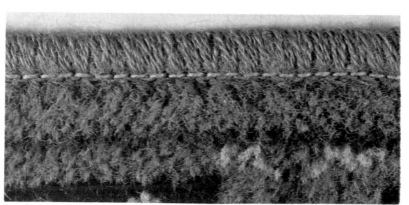

PLATE 108: *The machine-stitched overcasting on the side of a machine-made Oriental-design rug. Note the running stitch that secures the selvedge to the body of the carpet.*

EVALUATING CONDITION AND DETERMINING VALUE

The carpet as a whole must be specifically considered before making a detailed investigation of its component parts. If the colors and pattern are pleasing, then the potential buyer should check the carpet's structure.

EXAMINING THE OVERALL CARPET

Does the carpet lie flat on the floor? Wrinkles or ridges in the rug are caused by improper warp tension when woven and will not come out; they wear rapidly as well as appearing unsightly. Creases caused by the rug's being folded and a slight rippling of the selvedge, however, will come out over a period of time. Are the sides crooked, or are they relatively straight or parallel to each other? Some slight irregularities in the rug's sides are to be expected, but very crooked rugs are objectionable. Minor irregularities can be corrected by having the rug sized or stretched. This process should be done by the rug dealer before the rug is purchased. The rug should be carefully inspected afterward to ensure that the irregularities have been satisfactorily removed.

Each rug should be carefully inspected to make certain that no borders or portions of borders have been removed, especially the borders at the fringed ends of the rug. The same border designs should appear on all four sides of the rug (Turkoman rugs are the only exception, since they often have dissimilar side and end borders; see Turkoman Rugs, Chapter 6). The rug should not have been cut or shortened in any way.

The types of dyes and colors of the rug are the next consideration because of their effect on fading and running. Have or will the colors run together? Wiping a damp cloth over the top of a rug is a good test to determine if the rug is colorfast. A rug in which the dyes have already run should be obvious by the blurred design. By comparing the colors on the front and back of the rug, one can tell whether or not the rug has faded. The back of a faded rug will be much darker than the sunlight-faded front. Aniline dyes will have produced all of these undesirable features and rugs that have been colored with them should be avoided (see Chapter 2, pp. 24-25 for a discussion of aniline dyes).

STRUCTURE

Examining the structure of any rug is important; for a *used* rug it is essential. A used rug will have many opportunities to have been mistreated or cared for improperly. Many of the results of improper treatment are not immediately apparent on casual inspection.

In examining the structure of a rug, one must consider five major points. They are pile, warp and weft threads, fringe, selvedges, and knots.

PILE. The pile should be checked for worn areas, holes, and moth damage. Moth damage may appear on the top of the rug, the pile having been eaten down to the foundation; or it may be hidden on the back of the rug. The portion of the knot that is looped around the warp thread may also have been eaten. When this latter condition occurs, the pile is not secured to the foundation of the rug, and tufts of pile can be easily pulled out.

If the pile is well worn, the knots themselves are visible. Heavy traffic patterns may have caused the rug to be worn in spots, rather than uniformly over the entire surface.

If dead or skin wool (see Chapter 2, p. 21) has been used for the pile, the fibers will be brittle and will not wear well. In a used rug, worn spots caused by the dead wool will be quite obvious. In a new rug, dead wool can be felt by running one's hand across the pile; the dead wool has a definite coarse, bristly feel. Rugs have rarely been entirely woven of dead wool.

WARP AND WEFT THREADS. The warp and the weft threads should be checked for cuts and breaks. The rug should be turned completely over to facilitate this inspection. The cuts or breaks in the warp and weft threads can become serious if not repaired *before* the rug is purchased.

FRINGE. An inspection of the fringe should be made to determine if the fringe is the original, or if a replacement fringe has been added. Folding a rug back at the end of the pile is the best way to check whether the fringe is an unbroken extension of the warp threads. In a refringed rug the warp threads will terminate (either by being cut or turned under) and a fringed band attached. A refringed rug is less valuable than a rug with its original fringe, even if the original fringe is not in particularly good condition.

SELVEDGES. The selvedges bind the sides (terminal warp threads) of the carpet. They do not wear as quickly as the fringe, but do, on occasion, need to be reovercast, a process that should always be done by hand rather than machine.

KNOTS. The *jufti,* or false, knot has been used in some rugs in recent years. The knot is tied around four warp threads instead of the usual two. (See Chapter 2, p.22, *jufti* knot.)

KNOT COUNT

A construction variable basic to all Oriental rugs is the tightness of weave or "knot count." This is simply the number of knots in a given area (usually quoted as knots per square inch or centimeter), and may vary from as few as 20 to as many as 500 knots per square inch. The knot count can be an important tool in evaluating the quality of an Oriental rug—but only when it is properly used.

The assumption is too often made that "the tighter the knot count the more desirable or valuable the rug." Too many factors are involved for

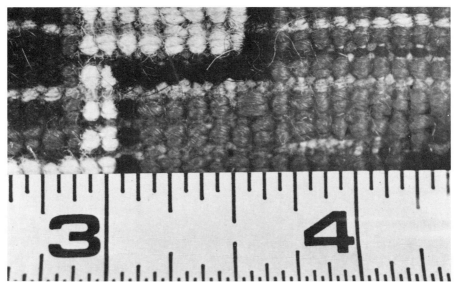

PLATE 109: *Counting knots per square inch.*

this statement always to be true. A Caucasian Shirvan rug, for example, will be more valuable than a Shiraz of the same age, condition, and knot count, because Caucasian rugs are more scarce. Each rug possesses its own attributes and is unique unto itself. Knot count should be used as a standard of quality only when comparing rugs from the same weaving center, condition, and age.

Knot count is calculated by counting the number of loops (knot backs) that fall within a one inch by one inch (one centimeter by one centimeter) square. Lay a ruler along a weft thread on the back of the rug; count the number of loops in an inch (centimeter). Turn the ruler along a warp thread and again count the number of loops in an inch (centimeter). Multiplying the two numbers together gives the number of knots per square inch (centimeter). This should be done in five different areas scattered over the back of the rug, and those results averaged. (See Plate 109.)

Rugs with higher knot counts have denser pile, which makes a sturdier, more durable rug. The pile is usually cut shorter, yielding a crisp design. These rugs are relatively more expensive than those with lower knot counts.

Each weaving center has its own characteristic range of knot counts. (See Appendix.) However, individual rugs from the same weaving center may vary widely in knot count.

Additional factors such as type of wool used and weaving techniques are variables that also affect the durability and quality of a rug. Knot count alone is not sufficient for making an evaluation of the quality or value of an Oriental rug.

Each of the points discussed does affect the value of a rug, and the price should reflect the rug's overall condition. A small flaw that might be objectionable to one person is not always objectionable to another. Since Oriental rugs are individually handcrafted, minor flaws will usually be found; absolute perfection should not be expected. If a rug has a deficiency, it is important that the purchaser be aware of the flaw and how it affects the rug's value; such information is necessary for an informed decision.

AGE

Rugs may be classified into three age-groups: new, semi-antique, and antique. A new rug is one that has never been used, although it can be several years old.

For practical purposes a semi-antique rug is from 25 to 50 years old and the antique rug is over 50 years old. Technically, a rug must be over 100 years old to be classified as an antique for U.S. customs purposes. Rugs which fall between the new and semi-antique classifications are termed "used." Their actual usage may vary considerably. The value of the used rug is generally less than its new and semi-antique counterparts, although it re-acquires value with age.

Age does affect the value of a rug, but age must be considered with condition. An antique rug which has been completely worn out is not valuable just because it is old. However, an antique rug in good condition can be priceless.

Bargaining

An Oriental rug may be purchased by making an offer lower than the stipulated or asking price, in much the same way as buying a house or a car. Bargaining is a compromise situation; in bargaining, knowledge is power. The final negotiated price can be strongly influenced by the knowledge of the buyer or seller.

Bargaining situations may be encountered almost any time a person is trying to buy an Oriental rug from an individual or a rug merchant. A rug dealer has certain costs that have been incurred, and his prices tend to reflect current market conditions; therefore, his ability and willingness to bargain is somewhat restricted. An individual's price may have been set rather arbitrarily because of lack of market information and his minimal investment in the rug (the rug may have been inherited or held for some time).

Knowledge in any situation makes the position of the buyer more certain and strategically sound. The more knowledgeable the buyer, the more likely the compromise will be in his favor.

Buying at Auctions

Many people are lured by the excitement of buying at auction. The hope of obtaining an Oriental rug for a fraction of its worth brings thousands of prospective buyers to auctions each year. The knowledgeable buyer may be able to make some good acquisitions, if he makes careful selections from the wide range of rugs offered.

Buying an Oriental rug at *any* auction entails risks; the type and degree of risk varies with the kind of auction and with the knowledge of the buyer. The successful buyer not only has knowledge of rugs, but also is familiar with the procedures and requirements of the auction. No rug purchased at an auction is returnable; the buyer rarely has any recourse if the rug is not as represented or is in need of repair, or if the buyer later decides that he does not like it. It is difficult to properly inspect the condition of a rug at auctions, and rugs are sold on an "as is" basis.

There are three types of auctions: traveling or itinerant; estate; and those held at established auction houses. Each has its own attributes and benefits, as well as disadvantages.

TRAVELING AUCTIONS

Traveling auctions go from city to city, selling Oriental rugs in motels or other rented facilities. The auctioneers are master showmen and may have shills (their hired people in the audience) to bid the price up until an acceptable level has been reached. The rug will not be sold for less than a predetermined price, which recovers all costs and yields a profit. Such costs include rent of the facility, auctioneer's commission, transportation costs, and initial investment in each rug.

A common misconception about the auction is that all rugs must be sold regardless of price. In the traveling auction, the auctioneer is under no such pressure; if bids do not exceed the auctioneer's minimum, that rug is withdrawn from consideration, to be offered again in the next city on the circuit. Because of all these considerations, the risk is placed on the potential buyer, not on the auctioneer. Only on rare occasions is one able to purchase a rug for an amount less than its worth.

Many of the rugs sold at traveling auctions are rugs that, for one reason or another, do not sell on the wholesale market, or are wholesaler's rejects. Importers buy in lots, rather than buying individual rugs; occasionally, pieces are encountered that do not meet the wholesale standard of quality. Many of these rugs find their way to the auction block. Not all rugs are inferior; a few good rugs are often deliberately interspersed among the others.

ESTATE AUCTIONS

In an estate auction the entire furnishings of a specific household are liquidated. Unlike the traveling auctioneer, the estate auctioneer has been commissioned to completely dispose of all items, and to get the most revenue possible. As a result, the potential buyer has a good chance to obtain a rug for less than its value. Yet risks are also present. In the traveling auction, the bidding is against the house; in the estate auction, one bids against other potential buyers, driving up the price. Rug dealers and other knowledgeable people are more apt to attend estate auctions, so competition can be fierce.

AUCTION HOUSES

Established auction houses have their reputations to maintain, as well as higher levels of costs to recover. The potential buyer not only bids against other bidders, but also against the house. The present owner of the rug to be sold has established the opening level for bids. Greater publicity usually attends the auctions of these houses, and collectors as well as dealers may come from afar.

Specialized collections and superior pieces are more likely to be offered by established auction houses because of their expertise, reputation, and ability to obtain the best possible prices for the owners. The prices obtained at these auctions will tend to reflect the actual worth of the rugs, and bargains should not be expected.

Knowledge is a prerequisite at any auction; ability to evaluate rug condition and knowledge of current prices and auction procedures are also vital. The buyer must be able to establish a realistic appraisal of the rug's worth on the market; he must also be able to set and observe a limit of the rug's value to him.

Care

Oriental rugs do not seem to absorb dirt the way machine-made commercial carpeting does. Even though dirt does not readily penetrate, soil will eventually work its way to the base of the pile. Rugs should be washed regularly, every three to five years, depending on the amount of traffic they undergo. Oriental rugs should never be chemically or steam cleaned, for these processes remove the natural oils and cause the pile to become brittle and wear more rapidly. Oriental rugs should be sent to a firm that specializes in cleaning them.

In vacuuming Oriental rugs, the vacuum cleaner should move in the same direction as the nap of the carpet lies. The direction of the nap can easily be determined by running the hand across the pile (from fringe to fringe). Vacuuming against the grain presses dirt back into the carpet. Never vacuum the carpet's fringe; sweep it with a broom. The continued catching of the fringe in the suction of a vacuum cleaner causes it to break and tear. Sweeping the carpet with a broom also helps bring out the natural patina, or sheen, in the rug.

Good-quality padding protects the rug, especially in heavily trafficked areas. The best padding is a hair- or fiber-filled pad with rubberized surfaces to keep the rug from moving or wrinkling. The life of an Oriental rug can be doubled with the use of a good-quality pad.

Spills of virtually any nature (from coffee to milk) may be removed without permanent stain if taken care of in time. Dilute the spill with plenty of water and blot the wet area until *all* of the moisture is removed. Failure to remove all of the moisture might result in mildew.

Moths can cause extensive damage to Oriental rugs. Not only do moths eat the pile, but they also eat the knots on the back of a rug. Moths are especially attracted to areas, such as those under furniture, that remain relatively undisturbed. It is quite simple to eliminate these pests and safeguard against their return. Both front and back of a carpet should be sprayed about every six months with any one of a number of moth sprays available on the market.

If a rug or carpet needs to be stored, it should be sprayed with moth spray, rolled, and put in a dry, moth-free environment.

As with any work of art, an Oriental rug must have proper care. Repairs may be necessary during the life of a rug; the fringed ends may need to be whipped or reinforced, and the selvedges may need to be overcast. Reweaving is even possible (to undo moth damage, for example), but should only be done by an expert, and should be attended to before the problem becomes serious and irreparable damage is done. Given proper care, a rug will last a lifetime or more.

APPENDIX

Summary Chart of Oriental Rugs,
by Availability, Durability, Price, Typical
Knot Count, and Common Rug Sizes

LEGEND: In the columns headed "Availability," "Durability," and "Price," the numbers express the relative availability, durability, and price of the rugs listed; a "1" indicates a rug that is *not* relatively available or durable, and is of *low* price. A "5" indicates a rug that is relatively widely available, is very durable, and of high price.

	AVAILABILITY	DURABILITY	PRICE	TYPICAL KNOT COUNTS					COMMON RUG SIZES		
				50–150	151–250	251–350	351–450	MORE THAN 450	2 X 4 OR SMALLER	3 X 5 TO 6 X 9	8 X 10 OR LARGER
IRAN											
Abadeh	2	4	4		x				x	x	
Afshar	1	3	3	x					x	x	
Arak/ Sultanabad	2	4	3		x						x
Ardebil	5	4	4			x			x	x	x
Balouchi	4	2	2	x					x	x	
Bibikabad	3	2	2	x							x
Bijar	1	4	4	x						x	
Dergazine	5	3	2	x					x	x	x

	AVAILABILITY	DURABILITY	PRICE	TYPICAL KNOT COUNTS					COMMON RUG SIZES		
				50–150	151–250	251–350	351–450	MORE THAN 450	2 X 4 OR SMALLER	3 X 5 TO 6 X 9	8 X 10 OR LARGER
Ferahan	1	3	4		x					x	
Hamadan	5	3	3	x	x				x	x	
Herez	5	3	3	x	x						x
Ingeles	3	4	3	x	x					x	
Isfahan	2	5	5			x	x			x	
Joshaghan	3	4	4		x	x				x	x
Karaja	4	4	3	x	x				x	x	
Kashan	4	4	4			x	x		x	x	x
Kerman	5	4	3		x	x			x	x	x
Kurd	2	4	3	x					x	x	
Lillihan	3	3	2	x	x				x	x	
Mahal	2	2	2	x							x
Malayer	2	3	3	x						x	x
Mashad	2	3	3		x					x	x
Meshkin	3	3	2	x						x	x
Nain	2	5	5			x	x		x	x	
Qashqai	2	3	4	x	x				x	x	
Qum	3	5	5			x	x			x	
Sarouk	4	4	4		x	x			x	x	x
Senna	1	4	4			x				x	
Seraband	4	3	3		x					x	x
Shiraz	4	2	3	x					x	x	x

	AVAILABILITY	DURABILITY	PRICE	TYPICAL KNOT COUNTS					COMMON RUG SIZES		
				50–150	151–250	251–350	351–450	MORE THAN 450	2 X 4 OR SMALLER	3 X 5 TO 6 X 9	8 X 10 OR LARGER
Tabriz	5	5	5		x	x			x	x	x
Yelemeh	4	3	4	x					x	x	
Yezd	1	4	4		x						x
CAUCASIAN											
Baku	1	3	5*	x	x					x	
Daghestan	1	3	5*	x						x	
Derbend	1	3	5*	x						x	
Gendge	1	3	5*	x						x	
Karabagh	1	3	5*	x						x	
Kazak	2	3	5*	x					x	x	
Kuba	2	3	5*	x	x					x	
Shirvan	2	3	5*	x	x					x	
Talish	1	3	5*	x						x	
New Caucasian rugs from USSR	1	3	4		x				x	x	
Turkoman											
Afghan	3	4	3	x					x	x	x

* Because most of the available Caucasian rugs are semi-antique or antique, very few will be found in excellent condition. All rug prices are strongly influenced by condition; rugs in excellent condition will bring top prices. Prices drop drastically for anything less than good condition.

	AVAILABILITY	DURABILITY	PRICE	TYPICAL KNOT COUNTS					COMMON RUG SIZES		
				50–150	151–250	251–350	351–450	MORE THAN 450	2 X 4 OR SMALLER	3 X 5 TO 6 X 9	8 X 10 OR LARGER
Daulatabad	2	4	4	x						x	
Ersari	1	3	4	x							
Khotan	1	2	3	x					x	x	
Mauri	2	4	4		x					x	x
Salor	1	4	4			x			x	x	
Sariq	1	3	4	x					x	x	
Tekke	2	3	4	x					x	x	
Yomud	2	3	4	x					x	x	
New Turkoman											
(Iran)	1	3	4	x					x	x	
New Turkoman											
(USSR)	1	3	4	x					x	x	
CHINA											
Peiking	4	3	3	x					x	x	x
Tientsin	4	3	3	x					x	x	x
PAKISTAN	5	3*	1*	x					x	x	x
INDIA	5	2*	1*	x					x	x	x

---

* Variations in durability and price are extreme, depending on quality. Index numbers should be regarded as an average only.

FOR FURTHER
READING

GENERAL

Dilley, A.U. *Oriental Rugs and Carpets*, rev. ed. by M.S. Dimand (New York: Lippincott, 1959).

Eiland, Murray L. *Oriental Rugs: A Comprehensive Guide* (Greenwich, Conn.: New York Graphic Society, Ltd., 1973). 196 pp.

Erdmann, Kurt. *Oriental Carpets* (Basingstoke, England: The Crosby Press, 1976).

Ferrero, Mercedes Viale (trans.). *Rare Carpets from East and West* (London: Orbis Books, 1972). 79 pp.

Formenton, Fabio. *Oriental Rugs and Carpets* (New York: McGraw-Hill, 1972). 252 pp.

Gans-Ruedin, E. *The Connoisseur's Guide to Oriental Carpets* (Rutland, Vt.: Tuttle, 1971). 431 pp.

Jacobsen, Charles. *Oriental Rugs* (Rutland, Vt.: Tuttle, 1962). 479 pp.

Larson, Knut. *Rugs and Carpets of the Orient* (London: Frederick Warne and Co. Ltd., 1966). 219 pp.

Liebetrau, Preben. *Oriental Rugs in Color* (New York: Macmillan, 1963). 131 pp.

Reed, Stanley. *All Color Book of Oriental Carpets and Rugs* (New York: Crescent Books, 1972). 72 pp.

Schlosser, Ignaz. *The Book of Rugs Oriental and European* (New York: Bonanza Books, 1963). 318 pp.

TURKOMAN

Azadi, Siawosch. *Turkoman Carpets* (Basingstoke, England: The Crosby Press, 1975). 129 pp.

Bogolyubov, Andrei Andreyevich. *Carpets of Central Asia* (Ramsdell, England: The Crosby Press, 1973). Edited by J.M.A. Thompson. 117 pp.

Leix, Alfred. *Turkestan and Its Textile Crafts* (Basingstoke, England: The Crosby Press, 1974). 53 pp.

O'Bannon, George W. *The Turkoman Carpet.* (London: Duckworth, 1974). 165 pp.

CAUCASIAN

Schurmann, Ulrich. *Caucasian Rugs* (Basingstoke, England: The Crosby Press, 1964). 142 pp.

PERSIAN

Edwards, A. Cecil. *The Persian Carpet* (London: Duckworth, 1953). 384 pp.

GLOSSARY

ABRASH   variation in a particular color resulting from the difference in dye lots.

ANATOLIAN   a name loosely applied to all Turkish rugs.

ARA-KHACHI   middle or main stripe in the border (*see* BALA-KHACHI).

AUBUSSON   a rug hand-woven in France, with a flat weave and pastel colors.

BAFF   knot.

BALA-KHACHI   small border stripe on either side of the main border stripe (*see* ARA-KHACHI).

BERDELIK   wall hanging; silk rugs generally fit into this category.

BID MAJNUM   weeping willow design, or a combination of weeping willow, cyprus, and poplar trees.

CARTOON   a piece of graphlike paper on which the rug pattern has been drawn; as a guide in weaving the rug, each square represents a single knot, the color of which is keyed to the color of the square (*see* TALIM).

CARTOUCHE   a cloudlike enclosure which surrounds a date or an inscription woven into a rug.

CAUCASIAN   refers to rugs woven in the Caucasus Mountain region. The patterns of these rugs are brightly colored, highly stylized, and geometrical.

CHUVAL   a large storage bag (*see* JUVAL).

DASGAH   loom.

DOZAR   refers to carpets 4 by 6 feet in size.

ENESSI   door (tent) drapery.

FRINGE   the loose ends of a carpet's warp threads emerging from the upper and lower ends of the carpet; it may be either knotted or plain.

GHALI   *see* KELLEI.

GHIORDES KNOT   Turkish knot; the knot encircles both warp threads.

GUL   Turkoman tribal emblem, which is unique to each tribe.

GULI   flower.

GULI HENNA   pattern with small yellow plant shape set in rows with profuse flower forms uniting them in a diamond arrangement.

HAMMAMLIK   bath rug.

HARSHANG   crab design; pattern with large motifs similar to the Shah Abbas pattern which suggest a crab.

HATCH   flower.

BEHBEHLIK   saddle bag or saddle cover.

HERATI   pattern that consists of a rosette surrounded by four leaves or "fish." The rosette is usually found inside a diamond shape (lozenge), although it need not be.

JUFTI KNOT   "false knot"; a modified Turkish or Persian knot, in which the weaver uses four warp threads per knot instead of two.

JUVAL   a tent bag (*see* CHUVAL).

KELEYGHI   small (5 by 10 to 6 by 12 feet) *kellei* used at the top of the Kellei Kenareh arrangement.

KELLEI   large, rectangular (6 by 16 to 8 by 20 feet) carpet used at the center of a traditional Persian room arrangement. (Also called "Ghali".)

KENAREH   runners (3 by 16 to 4 by 20 feet) used on either side of the *kellei*.

KHERDEH   outlines around patterns and designs on rugs.

KELIM   a pileless rug created by interweaving colored weft threads through the warp threads; or, a finished terminal portion of a carpet falling between the pile and the fringe.

KIABA   refers to a rug approximately 5½ by 9 feet in size.

LECHAI   corner design in a rug.

LECHEK TORUNJ   any design with corner and central medallions.

MAFRASH   large saddle bag.

MAKATLIK   long, narrow rugs; runners.

METNIH   main ground or field of a rug.

MIHRAB   arch or niche of a prayer rug.

MINA KHANI   design comprised of repeated floral motifs surrounded by four similar smaller flowers joined by vines to form a diamond arrangement.

MIR-I-BOTEH   design made of multiple rows of repeated *boteh* (pine cone or pears).

MORGI   "hen" pattern, an imaginative design resembling a chicken, which was originated by the Afshari tribe.

NAGZH   pattern (Persian).

NAMAZLIK   Namazi; prayer rug.

ODJAKLIK   hearth or fire rug.

PALAS   a Caucasian *kelim*.

PANEL DESIGN   design in which the field is divided into rectangular compartments, each of which encloses one or more motifs.

PATINA   the sheen acquired by the pile of the rug with age and use.

PERDE   refers to a rug approximately 5 by 9 feet in size.

PERSIAN KNOT   Senna knot; a strand of wool encircles one warp thread and winds loosely around the other.

PILE   nap of the rug; the clipped ends of the knotted wool.

PUSHTI   Persian small mat or pillow cover, approximately 2 by 3 feet.

SAFF   "family" prayer rug that has multiple *mihrabs* in a series.

SAVONNERIE   a rug hand-knotted in France, with a thick, heavy pile and pastel colors. New copies are now being woven in India.

SEDJADEH   medium-sized carpet, approximately 7 to 10 feet in length.

SELVEDGE   the sides of a carpet, which have been overcast with wool or cotton for reinforcement.

SENNA KNOT   Persian knot; encircles one warp thread and winds loosely around the other.

SHAH ABBAS   patron of carpet-making (A.D. 1571–1629); also the pattern with an all-over design with various types of palmettes, cloudbands, and vases interconnected by some form of stalk or tendril.

SU   lines dividing the border stripes.

TALIM   a piece of paper on which the design of a carpet has been written out, knot by knot. (Cf. *cartoon*.)

TEREH   design (Persian).

TEVEHR   band of solid color on the outside of a rug.

TORBA   storage bag.

TURBEHLIK   grave carpet, spread over graves as those in the West spread flowers.

This rug is the combined handiwork of every member of the household as an expression of sorrow.

TURKISH KNOT   Ghiordes knot; a strand of wool that encircles two warp threads, with the loose ends drawn tightly between the two.

TURKOMAN   rugs from the Turkistan regions; the pattern is made up of repeated *guls* (geometric motifs) that are specific to each tribe.

TORUNJ   a rug with a curved or floral medallion.

VESTIKLIK   Anatolian mat, used as a pillow cover.

WARP   threads running longitudinally through the fabric (anchored to the loom).

WEFT   threads running perpendicular to the warp (left to right).

YESTIK   Anatolian small mat or pillow cover.

ZARONIM   rugs approximately 3 by 5 feet in size.

ZARQUART   rugs approximately 2 by 4 feet in size.

ZIL-I-SOLTAN   "vase of roses" design; multiple rows of repeated vases of roses.

ZINJIR   chain; narrow stripe just inside the *tevehr*.

INDEX

Bold face numbers refer to illustration pages.